Know Better

Than Our Fathers

Ruwachemeth, LLC

Detroit, MI USA

Know Better Than Our Fathers
© 2022 Jason McGhee

Ruwach Emeth L.L.C.
ruwachemeth.org

ISBN 13: 979-8-9854109-3-8 (paperback)

Design by Christina Dixon

Printed in the United States of America

Know Better Than Our Fathers

"He filled me with words of truth that I may speak the same.

Like flows of waters, truth flows from my mouth,
and my lips reveal its harvest.

It gives me the gold of knowledge, for the mouth of the Lord is the true
word and the door of his light.

The highest one gave the words to his worlds which interpret his beauty,
recite his praise, and confess his thought as heralds of his mind and
instructors or his deeds.

The quickness of his words is unsayable, and like his statement it is sharp.
Its course knows no end and never fails. It stands.
Its descent and ways are incomprehensible.

Like his work is its end, which is the light and dawn of thought. Through it
worlds converse and the silent acquire speech.

From it came love and concord and candor, and
the word penetrated them and knew him who made it.

They came into concord.

The mouth of the highest one spoke to them, and that word made him clear.

The dwelling place of the word is you, and its truth is love.

Blessings on you who by it have learned everything
and have known the Lord in his truth."

Song 12 - Odes of Solomon

(Barnstone & Meyer, 2003,2009)

Table of Contents

Chapter 1: The Onion: Truth 4

Chapter 2: Foundations: Visitation................................15

Chapter 3: No Better: "Strange Fruit" 27

Chapter 4: The Purge...43

Chapter 5: Apocalypse..63

Chapter 6: True Repentance 83

Chapter 7: Spiritually Gentrified 93

Chapter 8: Turning the Corner..................................117

Chapter 9: Neo Pistis Sophia....................................129

Chapter 10: Me vs. My Image...................................137

Chapter 11: Know Better: Reframing 151

Works Cited..183

CHAPTER 1

The Onion: Truth

Would you do better if you knew better? How often have you said, "If I could do it all over knowing what I know now…"? While each day is an opportunity to demonstrate greater growth and maturity, we often don't get opportunities to stop and *gather ourselves*. Our progress and pace are largely dictated by our circumstances and environment, which is subjectively viewed by us and others. We often measure our progress through the acquisition of things, status, and power.

Because we have chosen the value of many of these things, over time our measurements have deviated from the one with the original design – Our Father. Living according to the plan of the ultimate architect of all things stands to make life much easier.

This necessitates a closer look at how we have come to learn about our creator and understand our own function. This is impossible without truth. Like an onion, truth has many layers. It's possible to have an onion in good condition with a layer inside completely rotten. Of course, you can't know the condition of the inner layers until you cut open the onion.

Clearly, with truth, this process is more complex. Quite often vantage points and perspectives can determine how we interpret what we see when we begin to dig deeper. Because we each have a variety of perspectives about the many things we observe, objective truth must be at the heart of all communications with the goal of mutual benefit and understanding. Often the question becomes one of trust and whether sources of truth are recognizable, reliable, and objective or not.

Having said all of that, great value is given to primary sources largely due to the lack of influence exerted by outside forces. It is quite difficult to assert authority over that which one knows through contact that is secondary or farther. Truths derived from observation alone can only be partial truths and there are rotten layers in our collective understanding of the Eternal, who is true, due to error.

The gospel of Christ is the knowledge that we can all have a primary relationship with our creator. Too often have the interventions of the Eternal been obscured by vessels whose contents have been unheard or ignored because of their plainness. Then others, without "godly authority," have dressed up and filled in the blanks of what they didn't understand or respect.

"But I fear, lest by any means, as the serpent beguiled Eve through his subtlety, so your minds should be corrupted from the simplicity that is in Christ."[1]

Why does this matter now? There is *"a rift between material and spiritual knowledge, with the one maimed, limp and doubting the existence of the other."* (Churton, p. 291) The relative truths that guide our choices are mingled with deliberate deceit. What are we left with when truth is "made manifest"? Are we strong enough to consider how our lives might change? Can we manage the damage to our pride individually and collectively while admitting we need to do better?

Have we ignored the obvious deficiency in our recognition or discernment? What is our rubric or process for deciphering the authenticity of divine inspiration? There have been so many that have exploited phrases such as, "God told me to tell you…" and "The Lord said.…" What helps us to distinguish between assertions of authority?

False claims and displays of authority have allowed documents and identities to change hands in ways that *have changed the truth into a lie.*[2] This includes the Doctrine of Discovery, the lynchpin of colonialism, which presents an example of the impact of a dysfunctional Christian theological imagination on social reality. We were warned this would happen many times and in many ways. *"It is to be regretted that*

---

[1] 2 Corinthians 11: 3 (The Open Bible)
[2] Romans 1:25

few of us have followed the wise advice and that many a priceless pearl, many a jewel of wisdom has been cast to an enemy unable to understand its value and who has turned around and rent us." (Blavatsky, 1877, p. 167)

Because many of our collective truths have been framed by those ignorant of their value, we have experienced a *gentrification[3] of faith and truth.* If history is told by the winners, in this case, I'm not sure we can identify the perpetrators of much genocide, rape, murder, violence, apostasy, etc. as winners. What have they truly won? Looking at the truth from the wrong perspective prevented the enemies of the Most High *and* his children from looking at their own truths from "his" perspective. Because the Father declared the end at the beginning, we can see how these events reveal efficacy in the fulfillment of his divine will.

The foundation of what we call Judaism was created with the story of the Exodus from Egypt of the Hebrews. However, the religion created using the Hebrew documents, Christianity, serves to reveal just how exponents can grow so large as to obscure their origins. Moses is recorded as having said,

"Happy art thou, O Israel, who is like unto thee; a people saved by the Lord, the shield of thy help, and who is the sword of thy excellency! And thine enemies shall be found

---

[3] gentrification - the process of conforming to an upper- or middle-class lifestyle, or of making a product, activity, etc., appealing to those with more affluent tastes

liars unto thee; and thou shalt tread upon their high places." [4]

The enemies of the Lord and the enemies of his people have endeavored to support a "new world order" without the *righteous* ways of the Lord and it has proven a snare to the nation of Israel brought to the United States in captivity. The beauty of all of this is that the "day of the Lord's vengeance" on any nation can occur whenever he decrees it. Whether we use Sodom and Gomorrah or Egypt as examples, we see how the Lord can judge a wicked nation, especially one that oppresses his people. This is, of course, if faith in the God of Abraham is truly something we really believe.

Difficult though it may be, staying focused on the task of uncovering the truth is the crux of my goal. While much learning can take place while reading this, there is a requisite level of knowledge that can make understanding easier. *"For nothing is secret that shall not be made manifest; neither anything hid that shall not be known and come abroad. Take heed therefore how ye hear; for whosoever hath, to him shall be given; and whosoever hath not, from him shall be taken even that which he seemeth to have."* [5]

I will focus on *impact and fulfillment*, which is more important to me than pointing fingers or assigning blame. *"This book, then, is not intended as a broadside against any particular person or class, but it is given as a corrective for methods which have not produced*

---

[4] Deuteronomy 33:29 (The Open Bible)
[5] Luke 8:17-18 (The Open Bible)

satisfactory results." (Woodson, p. 1) Throughout the course of this work I offer constructive critique and my suggestions for adjustments in practice.

I also want to snatch faith out of the teeth of religion and show that our fundamental conflicts are spiritual ones. Our Father, The Providence, the great invisible spirit, has been misunderstood and devotion to *him* taught in a non-spiritual way. This is a complex undertaking; "even to convey this general comprehension by mere language is a large, and by no means, an easy task. To pause at every moment of the exposition in order to collect what separate evidence may be available for the proof of each separate statement would be practically impossible. Such a method would break down the patience of the reader, and prevent him from deriving, as he may from a more condensed treatise, that definite conception as to what the esoteric doctrine means to teach, which it is my business to evoke." (Sinnet, p. 23)

Having quite a bit of information to synthesize I will use a combination of Eastern and Western methods in the process of this exposition. "The West pricks and piques the learner's controversial instinct at every step. He is encouraged to dispute and resist conviction. He is forbidden to take any scientific statement on authority. *Pari Passu[6]*, as he acquires knowledge, he must learn how that knowledge has been acquired, and he is made to feel that no fact is worth knowing, unless he knows, with it, the way to prove it a fact.

---

[6] *pari passu* – with equal pace or progress; side-by-side; without partiality

The East manages its pupils on a wholly different plan. It no more disregards the necessity of proving its teaching than the West, but it provides proof of a wholly different sort. It enables the student to search Nature for himself and verify its teaching, in those regions which Western philosophy can only invade by speculation and argument. It never takes the trouble to argue about anything, it says, "So and so is fact; here is the key of knowledge now go and see for yourself." In this way, it comes to pass that teaching *per se* is never anything else but teaching on authority. Teaching and proof do not go hand in hand; they follow one another in due order." (Sinnet, p. 22)

Because I am arguing that our *truths* concerning the *gospel message* have been given to us in error, I will lean toward the Eastern method. While I will show scriptural references that support my point of view, as I have already, I will avail myself of all *truths* as I believe truth is greater than that which can be found in one place.

As I reframe "the day" from the perspective of prophecy and scripture, what I present is simultaneously informational, rhetorical, philosophical, prophetic, and, I hope, even edifying and entertaining. As a music teacher, I use a spiral curriculum to approach content since all concepts are connected in their function. This exposition is patterned after this method, revisiting fundamental concepts repeatedly with greater depth and breadth throughout, just as there is unity in the spirit. Though I will repeat myself, each time I will add new perspective and information.

Because my goal is to expose and reclaim the truth of the gospel, I will begin with the promises in scripture once guarded by those called a nation of priests, the Israelites, or Jews. A great example of *why* I want and need to do this is given in the following excerpt of this story of the Beloved and his servant. I will refer to this quote from the book of Jacob Chapter 5 often as the portion I highlight here is related to the brief story found in Isaiah 5:1-7 about the Beloved and his vineyard.

"And it came to pass that Lord of the vineyard said unto his servant, "Let us go down into the nethermost parts of the vineyard and behold if the natural branches have also brought forth evil fruit." And it came to pass that they went down into the nethermost parts of the vineyard. And it came to pass they beheld that the fruit of the natural branches had become corrupt also; yea, and the first and the second and also the last; and they had all become corrupt. And the wild fruit of the last had overcome that part of the tree which brought forth good fruit, even that the branch had withered away and died. And it came to pass that the Lord of the vineyard wept and said unto the servant, "What could I have done more for my vineyard? Behold, I knew that all of the fruit of the vineyard, except these had become corrupted and now these which had once brought forth good fruit have also become corrupted and now all of the trees of my vineyard are good for nothing save to be hewn down and cast into the fire. And behold this last, whose branch hath

withered away, I did plant in a good spot of ground; yea, even that which was choice unto me above all other parts of the land of my vineyard. And thou beheldest that I also cut down that which cumbered this spot of ground, that I might plant this tree in the stead thereof. And thou beheldest that a part thereof brought forth good fruit, and a part thereof brought forth wild fruit; and because I plucked not the branches thereof and cast them into the fire, behold, they have overcome the good branch that it hath withered away. And now, behold, notwithstanding all the care which we have taken of my vineyard, the trees thereof have become corrupted, that they bring forth no good fruit; and these I had hoped to preserve, to have laid up fruit thereof against the season unto myself. But, behold, they have become like unto the wild olive tree, and they are of no worth but to be hewn down and cast into the fire and it grieveth me that I should lose them. But what could I have done more in my vineyard? Have I slackened my hand that I have not nourished it? Nay, I have nourished it, and I have digged about it, and I have pruned it and I have dunged it; and I have stretched forth mine hand almost all the day long, and the end draweth nigh. And it grieveth me that I should hew down all the trees of my vineyard and cast them into the fire that they should be burned. <u>Who is it that has corrupted my vineyard?</u> And it came to pass that the servant said unto his master, "Is it not the loftiness of thy vineyard — have not the branches thereof overcome the roots which are *good? And because the branches have overcome the roots thereof, behold they grew faster than the strength of the of the roots taking strength unto themselves. Behold, I say, is not this the cause that the trees of thy vineyard have become corrupted?" And it came to pass that the Lord of the vineyard said unto the servant, "Let us go to and hew down the trees of the vineyard and cast them into the fire, that they shall not cumber the ground of my vineyard, for I have done all. What could I have done more for my vineyard?" But, behold, the servant said unto the Lord of the vineyard, "Spare it a little longer." And the Lord said, "Yea, I will spare it a little longer, for it grieveth me that I should lose the trees of the vineyard. Wherefore, let us take of the branches of the these which I have planted in the nethermost parts of my vineyard, and let us graft them into the tree from whence they came and let us pluck from the tree those branches whose fruit is most bitter and graft them in the natural branches of the tree in the stead thereof. And this will I do that the tree may not perish, that, perhaps, I may preserve unto myself the roots thereof for mine own purpose."[7]*

I bear the responsibility of the servant to intercede before the coming destruction. My prayer has been that more of the truth be exposed so that honest choices can be made. Knowing that many of our choices have been made in

---

[7] Jacob 5:29-51 (The Book of Mormon, 1830)

ignorance and error, my hope is that truth – light will drive out the darkness created by lies and deceit and we can begin to heal and build.

As we begin this scriptural apocalypse[8], (unveiling of scriptural truths), I must acknowledge that this work is not at all comprehensive nor is it intended to be. Much has been uncovered over the years and compiling it all isn't necessary when one knows the source of truth. The most appropriate phrase to begin this journey is, "he that hath an ear, let him hear."

---

[8] apocalypse – any revelation or prophecy; unveiling

Foundations: Visitation

"For the vineyard of the Lord of hosts is the house of Israel, and the men of Judah his pleasant plant; and he looked for judgment, but behold oppression — for righteousness, but behold a cry."[9]

The verse above specifically defines what the vineyard of the Lord truly is – the house of Israel. Because "Israel" is scattered throughout the earth, its house is the entire world. As we go about to show how the Lord has been true to his word and his people, a picture of our current events can emerge.

The oppression and cry, spoken of in the verse above, come at the lack of judgment and justice in a nation where the Lord's people are captive. Egypt is the quintessential example of this and, yet the curse pronounced by Moses if the children of Israel didn't follow the commandments made this punishment clear:

"And the Lord shall bring thee into Egypt again with ships by the way whereof I spoke unto thee, thou shall see it no

---

9 Isaiah 5:7 (The Open Bible)

more again: and there ye shall be sold unto your enemies for bondmen and bondwomen, and no man shall buy you."[10]

The God of Israel made specific statements about Israel through Moses after delivering the children of Israel from Egypt. They entered a covenant with the Lord in which he gave them the choice of blessing or cursing due to their obedience to him. However, before Joseph died, after having been the vessel the Lord chose to preserve and add to the house of Israel, he let them know that God would bring them out of Egypt.[11]

The twenty-fourth verse of Genesis uses the word *visit* because Joseph first says that the Lord will *visit* you. Because the children of Israel were in Egypt and the Egyptians were oppressing them, the *visitation* of the Lord had severe consequences for Egypt. In scripture, we can identify where a "visitation" also represented a remembering of iniquity.

"Thus, saith the Lord unto this people, thus have they loved to wander, they have not refrained their feet, therefore the Lord doth not accept them; he will now remember their iniquity and visit their sins."[12]

---

[10] Deuteronomy 28:68 (The Open Bible)
[11] Genesis 50:24 (The Open Bible)
[12] Jeremiah 14:10 (The Open Bible)

A prophecy of the exile back to bondage or "Egypt" is given again by the prophet Hosea:

> *"They sacrifice flesh for the sacrifices of mine offerings, and eat it, but the Lord accepteth them not; now will he remember their iniquity and visit their sins — they shall return to Egypt. For Israel hath forgotten his Maker and buildeth temples; and Judah hath multiplied fenced cities. But I will send a fire upon his cities, and it shall devour the palaces thereof."[13]*

Over and over scripture recounts how the children of Israel perpetually transgressed the covenant with the Lord, they were then led into captivity and the Lord would release that captivity at the appointed time. But what of the nation that is also judged in the process?

In the case of the United States of America, this remembrance of iniquity[14] is quite easy to do since many of its past iniquities' impacts are growing exponentially and are helping to change the landscape of the entire population. What iniquities has the Lord discovered in the United States whose ways are as that of Sodom and Gomorrah?

> *"When I would have healed Israel, then the iniquity of Ephraim was discovered, and the wickedness of Samaria:*

---

[13] Hosea 8:13 (The Open Bible)
[14] iniquity – *aven* in Hebrew meaning to pant or exercise oneself, usually in vain; wickedness, crookedness (Strong, p. 309 see 205)

for they commit falsehood and the thief cometh in and the troop of robbers spoileth without. And they consider not in their hearts that I remember all their wickedness: now their own doings have beset them about; they are before my face."[15]

The Lord tells Moses to write and sing a song in the ears of the children of Israel as a witness for the Lord against the children of Israel. The Lord clearly declares,

"They have moved me to jealousy with that which is not God; they have provoked me to anger with their vanities and I will move them to jealousy **with those which are not a people***; I will provoke them to anger with a* **foolish nation***."* Later in the same song are the words, *"For they are a nation void of counsel, children in whom is no faith. O that they were wise, that they understood this, that they would consider their latter end!"*[16]

The United States is truly *not a people*. While it is certainly a collection of different people with different origins, cultures and identities, it is, above all, a divided people. The entire way we categorize and stereotype the citizens of the U.S. by race, ethnicity, gender, etc., perpetuates division and inequity. The

____

15 Hosea 7:1-2 (The Open Bible)
16 Deuteronomy 32:21; 28-29 (The Open Bible)

rampant use of precedence in the judicial system almost ensures that progress will be very slow in national justice.

> *"Then it was not enough for them to err about the knowledge of God, but though living in great strife due to ignorance, they call such great evils peace. For whether they kill children in their initiations, or celebrate secret mysteries or hold frenzied revels with strange customs, they no longer keep either their lives or their marriages pure, but they either treacherously kill one another, or grieve one another by adultery, and all is a raging riot of blood and murder, theft and deceit, corruption, faithlessness, tumult, perjury, confusion over what is good, forgetfulness of favors, defiling of souls, sexual perversion, disorder in marriages, adultery, and debauchery. For the worship of idols not to be named is the beginning and cause and end of every evil. For their worshipers either rave in exultation or prophesy lies, or live unrighteously, or readily commit perjury; for because they trust in lifeless idols, they swear wicked oaths and expect to suffer no harm. But just penalties will overtake them on two counts: because they thought wrongly about God in devoting themselves to idols, and because in deceit they swore unrighteously through contempt for holiness. For it is not the power of the things by which people swear, but the just penalty for those who sin, that always pursues the transgression of the unrighteous."[17]*

---

[17] Wisdom of Solomon 14:22-31 (The New Oxford Annotated Apocrypha Third Edition, 1989)

While the captivity of the children of Israel due to disobedience has always been devastating, the lands of captivity mostly represented places whose ways were not pleasing to the Lord. The song of the Lord to Moses says of this nation,

> *"For their vine is of the vine of Sodom, and of the fields of Gomorrah; their grapes are grapes of gall, their clusters are bitter. Their wine is the poison of dragons and the cruel venom of asps."* [18]

Contrary to popular belief, Sodom and Gomorrah had other ways that were abhorrent to the Lord than deviant sexual ones. The book of Jasher declares:

> *"And when a stranger came into their cities and brought goods which he had purchased with a view to dispose of there, the people of these cities would assemble, men, women, and children, young and old, and go to the man and take his goods by force, giving a little to each man until there was an end to all the goods of the owner which he had brought into the land. And if the owner of the goods quarreled with them saying, "What is this work which you have done to me?" Then they would approach to him one by one and each*

---

[18] Deuteronomy 32:32-33 (The Open Bible)

would show him saying, "I only took that little which thou didst give me." And when he heard this from them all, he would arise and go from them in sorrow and bitterness of soul, when they would all arise and go after him and drive him out of the city with great noise and tumult." [19]

In the book of Ezekiel is written,

"Behold, this was the iniquity of thy sister Sodom, pride, fullness of bread and abundance of idleness was in her and in her daughters, neither did she strengthen the hand of the poor and needy. And they were haughty and committed abominations before me, therefore, I took them away as I saw good." [20]

The iniquity of the United States is quite similar to that which is described in the above passage. Having been born and raised here in one of the created "ghettos" of America, I've lived the "American way" firsthand, and it can be difficult to maintain moral ground. Living life as a by-word[21] definitely has its drawbacks and being treated as an inferior, criminal practically everywhere you go is hard on the psyche.

But we ALL, as citizens, are prey for the rich corporations whose dollars have helped to create a state of

---

[19] Jasher 18:16-17 (Johnson, 2008)
[20] Ezekiel 16:49-50 (The Open Bible)
[21] *By-word* is used in the Torah to describe the reproach of being referred to by a name other than that which accurately describes one's identity. Nigga and spic are examples of by-words.

dependency and poverty. This poverty has been the breeding ground to fulfill all the pronouncements of the curses Moses gave that are recorded in Deuteronomy; the rampant injustice is also part of the punishment.

Our collective action doesn't show that we understand that our behavior is tied not only to the remnant of Israelites brought to the United States in captivity, but this *visitation* is also tied to faith and the "ways" of the United States and its affiliates.

Though there is no official religion in the United States, Christianity and the use of the Bible are intimately woven into the fabric of civic interaction. Presidents and other government officials are sworn in using the Bible and prayer is a regular activity in the civic sphere. Though the United States Constitution forbids the laws' support for the practice of any specific religion, these norms negate the efficacy of that law.

This amorality extends throughout the law. I had the pleasure of being a legal assistant for a criminal defense attorney and there I learned just how much the legal system is arrayed against its citizens in many US cities. The traffic stop has become a pretext through which racial profiling is executed. Michelle Alexander's *The New Jim Crow* highlighted and expounded on the perpetuation of injustice in America with details and its data is outdated now. It's no accident that deliberate injustice contributes immensely to the lopsided application of the law in the criminal justice system.

Unfortunately, even with detailed, specific data, there seems to be little appetite for true justice. I've lost count of how many police officers have been acquitted after killing an unarmed black man or a person of color that had committed a crime punishable by a fine. The due process occurs more transparently, and maybe even effectively when there is independent evidence demonstrating the undeniable truth of misconduct and it is made public independent of the justice system and media.

And while efforts to change these facts are decades old, even with the commitment to non-violence articulated so eloquently by Dr. King, efforts are met with police brutality and political gamesmanship. There are even efforts by extremists to commit revolutionary anarchy. Another civil war is not what we need!

> "… there is weakness in this method because it ends up creating many more social problems than it solves. And I am convinced that the Negro succumbs to the temptation of using violence in its struggle for freedom and justice, unborn generations will be the recipients of a long and desolate night of bitterness. And our chief legacy to the future will be an endless reign of meaningless chaos." (Washington, pp. 44-45)

We as children of the Most High have been so angry at the citizens of the United States, but shouldn't we be angry with ourselves? We wouldn't be here if we had obeyed, and things won't improve until we repent. Haven't we learned how merciful and gracious the Lord is or do we not love him?

As rich as the United States is, does it realize the true source of its wealth? We've lost our faith in the Most High and the benefit of being honest. Lack of this knowledge is indeed why the people of the Lord are continually destroyed. We, as people of true faith, are living a double life in many ways.

> "From the double life every American Negro must live, as a Negro and as an American, as swept on by the current of the nineteenth while yet struggling in the eddies[22] of the fifteenth century, from this must arise a painful self-consciousness, an almost morbid sense of personality and a moral hesitancy which is fatal to self-confidence…Such a double life, with double thoughts, double duties, and double social classes must give rise to double words and double ideals, and tempt the mind to pretense or to revolt, to hypocrisy or to radicalism." (Dubois, p. 122)

We have been complicit in making ourselves perpetual prey. If we are destroyed for lack of knowledge, won't we

---

[22] eddy – a small whirlpool

continue to be destroyed if we reject the knowledge that the Father is giving? What if this rejection of the knowledge of the Lord's ways is due to *pleasure in unrighteousness*? Has the "light" of today been shown to be darkness and the people choose to remain in darkness? It is written that the word of the Lord is truth and truth is light.[23] What, then, is the darkness? What are the lies?

Indeed, several lies are lived out daily in the United States. There are truths that have become lies in practice because of ignorance and misunderstanding.

Just Blame Me

There are the lies of those whose intent is to deceive
that speak words of truth that they don't understand or believe.
Then there are the impostors who hate and lie,
They deceive and spy all the while they tell you they love you and
they're on your side.
Only the true light of truth can rescue us
from the web of lies that has us tangled up.
Who's to blame for all the lies and deceit?
That answer is so hard, **just blame me!**
Maybe we could move forward if we did that.
At least maybe then we'd stop looking back.
We might look to the Lord and then we'd see,
It was all in the plan for you and me.
Moses said it a long time ago, but let's be clear,

---

23 Gospel of John 17:17 (The Open Bible)

didn't Abraham know?
We keep getting boundaries that are soon erased.
The Father above gave us truth and grace.
So why do we keep going back?
The truth is there's something in us that lacks!
The truth is that; God is good.
But someone messed things up with should.
"You should have all of this by now!"
"Why are you kneeling? You should bow."
"Why do you sprinkle? You should immerse."
And deacon, "Why are you reading that verse?
Read this one instead; you should already know."
"After they hear this, they will give and go."
We've become entangled again in bondage you see
When we are promised life more abundantly.
That doesn't mean we get more stuff.
It really means we share more love.
Not lust – Not sex – Not covetousness
But agape – true love!
That's what's best!

- J. McGhee

CHAPTER 3

No Better:
"Strange Fruit"

Our great loss as a society is the loss of faith, truth, and spirituality. "Spirituality is not blind faith about things invisible. It is an inspired use of things known and available. That man is religious who lives well. That man is sacrilegious who perverts universal good for purposes of private gain." (Hall, 2008, p. 51) This journey in a land without faith based in truth has dulled our senses to what the Lord requires of *us*. Serious faith and spirituality can lead to great productivity when coupled with the truth.

What, then, is the function of a true prophet in a society that despises the ways of the Lord and views spiritual principles as archaic? As a public-school teacher, I have seen so many students become textbook underachievers, me included, because of the rampant, dangerous treatment of those who excel academically or morally. It's actually popular to be mediocre in America and virginity is considered foolish more often than not! Consider the pride, hopelessness and ignorance highlighted in the lyrics to *Gangsta Paradise*, made famous by Coolio, that reveals the upside-down nature of some of our judgment of what is good versus what is evil.

As I walk through the valley of the shadow of death
I take a look at my life and realize there's nothin' left
'Cause I've been blastin' and laughin' so long that
Even my momma thinks that my mind is gone
But I ain't never crossed a man that didn't deserve it
Me be treated like a punk, you know that's unheard of
You better watch how you talkin' and where you walkin'
Or you and your homies might be lined in chalk
I really hate to trip, but I gotta loc
As they croak, I see myself in the pistol smoke

In this "melting pot" of culture and faith practice, how do we apply spiritual principles? Are we so busy trying to understand and relive yesterday that we can't apply what we learn from it today? Or is it just that we haven't really learned, only observed and imitated? So, what do we really know? How "true" is our knowledge? Have we *known* or planned so much that we have no room to act on new or newly understood information?

The rigidity of many of our systems and processes reveals a need to reposition our knowledge and skills to be responsive and effective — not just stable. In fact, a lack of responsiveness and efficacy actually represent instability and danger of collapse. The image must be one with the essence; too often *we've* accepted what looked and felt good though it was not actually good for us.

Our Father is more than capable of maintaining the complexity of our liberty whether we have chosen him or not. The question is: who are we when our truth and innocence are reclaimed? What must we shed to grow? The Father is best at revealing *his* perspective of things; so, what do we do to help ourselves? After repentance, I believe we must address our *attrition of faith*. Attrition can partially be defined as 1) a rubbing away or wearing down by friction; 2) a gradual diminution in number or strength due to constant stress, or 3) repentance for sin motivated by fear or punishment rather than by love of God.

Some of our *attrition of faith* is due to the condition of captivity. The conditions that usually persist during captivity can produce more than one result. However, captivity isn't as much punishment from the Lord as it is his chastisement and turning away his face, which results in a loss of some of *his* protection. Often, the ways of other nations are so contrary to the ways of the Lord that being subject to them can be difficult. But the difficulty is only for those that know what is truly missing.

Those without true faith lack the scruples to avoid spiritual forms of oppression. Quite often, they're unable to recognize the deficiencies in their own forms of wisdom and spiritual understanding. The church, under the leadership of the papacy with the strength of the Roman government, has perpetuated these deficiencies of understanding and created an entire system of ways that has grown up with the true vine, but itself represents a degenerate plant.[24]

> "It gave theological permission for the European body and mind to view themselves as superior to the non-European bodies and minds. The doctrine created an insider perception for the European while generating an outsider other; it created an identity for African bodies as inferior and only worthy of subjugation; it also relegated the identity of the original inhabitants of the land "discovered" to become outsiders, now unwelcome in their own land. (Charles & Rah, p. 21)

Those who stole the land now claimed power over those who originally held the land. In order to strengthen the claim to usurped land, the more pure, European-American Christian settler colonialists needed to elevate themselves over and against the indigenous inhabitants. The dominant powers created dysfunctional narratives derived from a diseased social and theological imagination that elevated the sense of worth of the dominant group. This lie of supremacy empowered the

---

[24] Jeremiah 2:21 (The Open Bible)

dominant group to define the other as inferior and claim authority over them." (Charles & Rah, p. 21)

Unfortunately for the church, it has imitated and stolen the identity of an unfaithful, wandering people and has adopted the good and bad without the truth to distinguish between the two. To advance its own authority, the church sought to define secrets that were given to Israel. "For example, the basic assumption that the interpretation of the Old Testament was exclusively the prerogative of the Church, linked with the normalization of the allegorical method, led to the neglect of the Hebrew world view. This resulted in theological thought being set in an essentially Greek philosophical frame of reference." (Diprose, p. 3) More importantly, the *Christian* church has done this though Christ, its namesake, said that salvation is of the Jews.[25]

But what could I have done more in my vineyard? Have I slackened my hand that I have not nourished it? Nay, I have nourished it, and I have digged about it, and I have pruned it and I have dunged it; and I have stretched forth mine hand almost all the day long, and the end draweth nigh. And it grieveth me that I should hew down all the trees of my vineyard and cast them into the fire that they should be burned. <u>*Who is it that has corrupted my vineyard?*</u>"[26]

---

[25] Gospel of John 4:22 (The Open Bible)
[26] Jacob 5:47 (The Book of Mormon, 1830)

The above-quoted passage is an excerpt from the passage from the book of Jacob quoted in chapter one with the emphasis here on the condition of the fruit of the vineyard. The Lord of the vineyard laments over the time and effort spent in the vineyard that still yielded corrupt fruit. This passage ends with a rhetorical question because the Lord of the vineyard is well aware of who has corrupted the vineyard. (I blame false doctrine and apostasy; greed, ambition for wealth, and vanity were probably in on it too.) Because we know that the vineyard of the Lord is the house of Israel who is scattered, the corruptors come from inside and out, which includes the church.

The scriptures are full of examples that show the different nations that attempted to plunder Israel; some of those nations were successful and others weren't. Even after all the signs and wonders done before the exodus of the children of Israel, Egypt pursued and was defeated because El Shaddai, GOD ALMIGHTY fought for them.[27] This threat to nations was one of the strong influences that created jealousy and malice toward Israel. As the children of Israel travelled through the wilderness the Lord tells them:

"This day will I begin to put the dread of thee and the fear of thee upon the nations that are under the whole

---

[27] Deuteronomy 1:30 (The Book of Mormon, 1830)

heaven, who shall hear report of thee, and shall tremble and be in anguish because of thee."[28]

Unfortunately, if we were to look back closely, we would see that this same jealousy and envy began between brothers. Family turmoil, which can be traced back to Cain and Abel, has created much of the vengeance and jealousy that has grown exponentially and impacted the landscape of the world.

Israel as a nation was chosen as a nation of priests, which did not negate the God-given inheritances of the other nations. This nomadic, nation was supported by the Almighty precisely because they were and are the Lord's peculiar treasure.[29] Because of the idolatrous ways of the other nations, they often misunderstood the source of the Israelites' strength, which didn't come from any particular *thing*. They did not choose the Lord, he chose the line of Abraham, which included them, deliberately. Moreover, the children of Israel, who were multiplied in Egypt, were the recipients of the oath made to Abraham and his descendants.

"The Lord did not set his love upon you, nor choose you because you were more in number than any people. But because he would guard the oath which he had sworn unto your fathers, has the Lord brought you out with a mighty hand, and redeemed you out of the house of bondmen, from the hand of Pharoah, King of Egypt. Know, therefore, that

---

[28] Deuteronomy 2:25 (The Open Bible)
[29] Exodus 19:4-5 (The Open Bible)

the Lord, he is God, the faithful God, which guards his covenant and mercy with them that love him and guard his commandments to a thousand generations; and repays them that hate him to their face to destroy them. He will not be slack to him that hates him, he will repay him to his face."[30]

The Lord extends his hand through *earthen vessels* that seek to do his will. The part I think is grossly misunderstood now is the Lord's characterization of the work of the assembly and holy things as iniquity.[31] Because of the lack of understanding of those who falsely claim spiritual authority, great apostasy has been perpetuated. It was the nation of Israel that the Lord chose to disclose his word, statutes, and judgments,[32] others never knew them.

This attempt to understand and even teach the ways of the Lord, whom they didn't know, just by reading the documents of some of his people created a vacuum of truth and understanding. This is precisely why it is necessary to understand *replacement theology*.

"The claim to have completely replaced Israel in God's plan or, more often, to be the reality of which Israel had only been the type, led the Church to discriminate against all things

---

[30] Deuteronomy 7:7-10 (The Open Bible)
[31] Exodus 28:38 (The Open Bible); Numbers 18: 1-2 (The Open Bible)
[32] Psalm 147:19-20 (The Open Bible)

Jewish, except those things that she herself had taken over. Among the latter were the sacred writings which God had entrusted to Israel and which contain explicit commands against iconography. We have seen that the practice of allegorical interpretation permitted the Church to neglect the clear teaching of scripture when this did not agree with current theological opinion, which explains why the Medieval Church ignored the prohibition of icons in the books of Moses, the Hebrew prophets, and Paul's letter to the Romans. The authorized use of images came to be so common that those who opposed the practice were thought to be guilty of grave error while those supporting them were considered orthodox!" (Diprose, p. 167)

The attempt to fill the vacuum of their ignorance has exposed their lack of true, practicable faith. How can you profess to teach that which you do not know? There is a difference between teaching and giving the answers. Those who receive the answer to the question are not the same as those who have learned the information. Learners can apply knowledge; those that heard the "right answer" still know nothing but their ability to appear knowledgeable. If the concept comes up, they're often unable to act appropriately or apply the information in context.

How much confusion has been caused by the misappropriation of information containing spiritual mysteries? Exposing a mystery doesn't seem to honor the sacredness of it. Sacred mysteries of faith and spirituality have been guarded over time to protect them from misuse and abuse. Still, the wicked and greedy have sought to benefit personally from that which was created to benefit all.

So, what if you receive incorrect answers? Because you haven't learned or known the truth, you are at risk of your theft and cheating being the evidence that you stole and cheated. What if this is the reprobate mystery spoken of in chapter sixteen of the book of Enoch? This is also referred to where it says in Psalm 69:

> *"Let their table become a snare before them: and that which should have been for their welfare, let it become a trap. Let their eyes be darkened, that they see not.... they persecute him whom you have smitten; and they talk to the grief of those who you have wounded. Add iniquity unto their iniquity and let them not come into your righteousness."[33]*

---

[33] Psalm 69:22-27 (The Open Bible)

How can a structure for true worship be created by those who reject the truth?

The founding of a Christianity that doesn't follow Christ *in truth* was destined to fail. *"Except the Lord build the house, they labor in vain that build it; except the Lord keep the city, the watchman wakens but in vain."*[34] How do you follow someone you cannot see? What does it look like to serve in a kingdom that is only partially visible? How can a structure for *true* worship be created by those who reject the truth? *"…But the hour comes, and now is, when the true worshippers shall worship the Father in spirit and in truth."*[35]

How do we access our spirit to use it for worship? If we know how to access and use our spirit, only we and the Lord of ALL spirits know the truth of our motives and intentions. If those of us who truly possess this freedom use it to manipulate others, are others able to worship freely? Aren't those being manipulated tools of others' worship? If our Father is worshipped because of fear, ignorance, compulsion or manipulation, is that worship done *in truth* or does it too represent an *attrition of faith*? Is this worship acceptable to him?

If grace and truth came by Jesus Christ[36] and his life and sacrifice were acts of the Father's love[37], have we rejected the

---

[34] Psalm 127:1 (Et Cepher 3rd Edition)
[35] Gospel of John 4:22-23 (The Open Bible)
[36] Gospel of John 1:17
[37] Gospel of John 3:16

Father's love by omitting the truth? Can we truly follow someone whose words and admonitions we reject? Furthermore, how can we follow one in whose direction we avoid traveling?

We have chosen to accept current practices without an understanding of what Christ said and did. Though most of us were born into it, we have heard messages redefining Christ's message as somehow different than his Hebrew predecessors. Christ clearly declared that his existence was tied to fulfilling the Torah not destroying it. [38]

Without true knowledge and understanding of the Lord's idea of a priesthood, which was given to the nation of Israel exclusively[39], the church has become exactly what the priesthood it imitates was prophesied to become. Much of the priesthood and service of the Lord were given to the sons of Aaron and the tribe of Levi. Again, the Lord describes the service of the Levites as iniquity because part of the service of the sanctuary is to bear the iniquities of the people.

The Levites were scattered amongst all the tribes but received no inheritance because they inherited the holy things and their relationship with the Lord. [40] The Levites' and Israel's violation of the covenant and work of the sanctuary including perversion of the tithe, ways of admission, etc. were foretold

---

[38] Matthew 5:17
[39] Psalm 147:19-20
[40] Numbers 18:20-24 (The Open Bible)

by Levi at his death. These are the people that the *iniquity of the holy things* was stolen from.

> *"Yea, ye shall bring a curse upon our race, because the light of the law which was given for to lighten every man; this, ye desire to destroy by teaching commandments contrary to the ordinances of God. The offerings of the Lord we shall rob, and from* **His** *portion shall ye steal choice portions, eating them contemptuously with harlots. And out of covetousness ye shall teach the commandments of the Lord. Wedded women shall ye pollute, and the virgins of Israel shall ye defile; and with harlots and adulteresses shall ye be joined, and the daughters of the Gentiles shall ye take to wife, purifying them with an unlawful purification and your union shall be like unto Sodom and Gomorrah. And ye shall be puffed up because of your priesthood, lifting yourselves up against men, and not only so, but also against the commands of God. For ye shall contemn the holy things with jests and laughter. Therefore, the temple, which the Lord shall choose, shall be laid waste through your uncleanness and ye shall be captives throughout all nations. And ye shall be an abomination unto them, and ye shall receive reproach and everlasting shame from the righteous judgment of God."*[41]

---

[41] Testament of Levi 4:15-21 (The Lost Books of the Bible and the Forgotten Books of Eden, 1926; 1927)

"And ye shall make void the law and set at nought the words of the prophets by evil perverseness. And ye shall persecute righteous men and hate the godly; the words of the faithful shall ye abhor. And a man who reneweth the law in the power of the Most High, ye shall call a deceiver; and at last ye shall rush upon him to slay him, not knowing his dignity, taking innocent blood through wickedness upon your heads. And your holy places shall be laid waste even to the ground because of him. And ye shall have no place that is clean; but ye shall be among the Gentiles a curse and a dispersion until **HE** *shall again visit you, and in pity shall receive you through faith and water."*[42]

These are some of the foundations of what we call church today. But not all those that have gained acclaim due to their teaching and built churches in their own names are unrighteous, but its exponential growth has encouraged *the corrupt fruit to overcome the good branch* as is represented in the parable above, and now, all the fruit has been corrupted.

Because the reach of the Church is large and it, though severely divided, is one of the primary standards by which morality is measured, it represents a false weight and measure because of the lack of truth and understanding in Church doctrine. Often, those who have become pastors and teachers suffer from the same "heart condition" as the sons of Levi.

---

[42] Testament of Levi 4:25-29 (The Lost Books of the Bible and the Forgotten Books of Eden, 1926; 1927) bolded word represents Author emphasis

"They win disciples who put implicit faith in them, and found their little school, which flourishes for a time within its own limits; but speculative philosophy of such a kind is rather occupation for the mind than knowledge." (Sinnet, p. 10)

Are we able to live honestly and objectively using knowledge, wisdom, and faith in the Father through our experience walking with him? Or, are we busy repeating the patterns we learned without understanding because we've trusted others?

CHAPTER 4

The Purge

"By mercy and truth, iniquity is purged: and by the fear of the Lord men depart from evil."[43]

The Lord God is the same yesterday, today, and forever. As his servants, especially those with the responsibility of the holy things, our responsibility is to care for *the least*: the fatherless, widows, oppressed, needy, naked, injured, blind, lame, old, and young. Were we to have truly lived up to this charge, the Lord would have added to us, and still has allowed some prosperity despite our collective unfaithfulness.

But the pursuit of wealth and compensation fueled by ambition must take a backseat to true service. Ambition without principle is an exercise in vanity; we must be sure of the principles we live by. Quite often the populations I've described cannot even afford the help they need. Our job is to enrich the people and not ourselves.

Herein lies the necessity for honest, principled God-fearing public servants. Sacrifice and service in spirit and truth honor the gospel better than wealth and status. We can glorify our Father and honor the words of his servants best by being

---

43 Proverbs 16:6 (The Open Bible)

the best at what he created *us* for. That, after all, is how a body works; everything does its part.

It doesn't work as well when our *less comely* parts are rejected for being different. All parts matter and work best when they operate as intended. This is the Church's achilles heel! Very often, leaders of churches see people through the lens of where they might fit in the church's institutional structure NOT who they really are or how the creator uniquely endowed them to serve in *his* kingdom.

The Church fueled by Christian doctrine has become like trying to tell time using a clock without batteries. We must live out our lives in *our own* truth. Appropriately applying spiritual principles requires using the correct tools at the right time. Just like medicine though, the patient matters. Perpetual misunderstandings of people and spiritual conditions have led to the wrong treatments being given to the wrong *patients*. Great spiritual harm, which can result in a spiral of decline, can be done inadvertently due to ignorance. *"The medicines required for healing differ according to the difference of the disease, and many a medicine is beneficial to one patient and harmful to another."* (Al-Ghazali A. H., 2010, p. 11)

Just a quick reminder: my goal here is a *truthful* reframing of the times from the perspective of those waking up in captivity as those who once possessed the responsibility of care for the righteous priesthood of the Most High. The Church is not and does not represent the righteous priesthood of the God of Abraham, Isaac, and Jacob though his prophets may be working within it. The gentrification performed by the church, however, is proof of their belief in the influence of true faith in the power of the Father as taught by Christ. Apparently, they thought, by stealing documents containing truth, they could assume the responsibility of guarding that truth.

> *"We should not be ashamed to acknowledge truth and to assimilate it from whatever source it comes to us, even if it is brought to us by former generations and foreign peoples. For him who seeks the truth, there is nothing of higher value than truth itself; it never cheapens or abases him who searches for it but ennobles him and honours him."* (Al-Ghazali I. , 2016, p. 22)

If theirs had been a noble search for truth and an attempt to commune with the God of the Hebrews, the Church may have been able to remain. As long as the institution called Church stands opposed to the truth, with lies, deceit, and apostasy, it dooms itself to destruction through the loss of credibility. Because interspersed throughout history are true believers, truth has been infused into this false system, though rejected, but time has calcified the falsehood so that many won't acknowledge truth because it is unrecognizable.

This too is part of the punishment of captivity; Moses forewarned the children of Israel of this specifically. And, while appearing to sound critical of the church, the constructive, prophetic criticism I provide is no different than that which has been articulated in the books of Moses, the Psalms, and the writings of the prophets.

If we truly have faith, we can acknowledge when the Lord confronts us about our behaviors and recognize his chastisement as love beyond that which our flesh and blood can know. Confrontation is not condemnation. We can also accept the punishment for our transgressions knowing that it doesn't reduce the Lord's faithfulness for us to be punished. It also doesn't absolve us from choosing to truly walk in his ways even in the place of exile.

The question we must ask ourselves and our leaders going forward is: have we truly searched for the Father or have we investigated what he said to control others? Moreover, does Christian doctrine still attempt to put the will of the Father first? In some outgrowths of Christianity, the doctrine teaches that God wants us to have what we think we want and need despite known truths. Unbelief is not characterized by an inability to believe <u>for</u> things, but an inability to believe <u>in</u> the Father.

The Christian *doctrinal reframing* of faith has allowed money and access to drive systems that teach universal truths as capitalist markets causing the human psyche to be manipulated through deceit. In this way, the applicability of true spiritual principles is diluted through the pursuit of superficial productivity.

> "The danger of all systems is that they tend to mistake the words, which serve as pointers, for the realities to which they point. ... We must be extremely careful that we do not earmark terms as known because named, thus depriving ourselves of authentic knowledge." (Hoeller, pp. 34-35)

While there appears to be success on the surface which can be an indicator of healing, the spirit and heart are, or can be, severely ill. It is, therefore, not good to judge people by *things* or to judge *things* by people. Furthermore, if we are made in his image, the flesh is but a shadow. Shouldn't we be constantly trying to imitate the source of our existence? Sometimes it seems we want the one who is superior to aid our pursuit of inferiority and superficial adulation. What do we do with our invisible parts that are truly more like him?

The events highlighted so far throughout this work allude to various levels of the fulfillment of prophecies contained in various scriptures. The combination of various areas of fulfillment as they are tied together in the case of the United States AND the Church create the perfect scenario for trial with judgment according to the **TRUTH** of what we've done from the perspective of the Lord. Christ explains it this way:

"And this is the condemnation, that light is come into the world, and men loved darkness rather than light, because their deeds were evil. For everyone that does evil hates the light, neither comes to the light, lest his deeds should be reproved. But he that does truth comes to the light, that his deeds may be made manifest that they are wrought in God."[44]

The activities of those who hate the Lord and his ways are both deliberate and done in ignorance. Christ said, *"And these things they will do unto you because they have not known the Father nor me."[45]* This lack of knowledge of the Father is exposed by the perpetual ignorance and vanity of mankind. My hope is that knowledge of these revelatory truths will aid in our common purification.

"Thus saith the Lord, Let not the wise man glory in his wisdom, neither let the mighty man glory in his might, let not the rich man glory in his riches: But let him that glorieth glory in this that he understandeth and knoweth me, that I am the Lord which exercise lovingkindness, judgment, and righteousness, in the earth: for in these things I delight, saith the Lord. **Behold, the days come, saith the Lord, that I will punish all them which are circumcised with the uncircumcised;** *Egypt,*

---

44 Gospel of John 3:19-21 (The Open Bible)
45 Gospel of John 16:3 (The Open Bible)

and Judah, and Edom, and the children of Ammon, and Moab, and all that are in the utmost corners that dwell in the wilderness: for all these nations are uncircumcised, and all the house of Israel are uncircumcised in the heart." [46]

Truth is greater than can be contained in one body of writings and it can be found in many places. Can the "builders of the wall" acknowledge the "untempered mortar" that has held it up? Did the Lord truly build this house or just allow it to be built? Part of the problem with Christianity, which will be discussed in detail, is the attempt to limit the eternal nature of the Father's will with the chronology of history.

The concepts and principles that governed the people that *walked with God* are beyond time as the Father is. In this way, the Father's will must not be falsified or faked, especially not deliberately. Counterfeit operations of his spirit can be defined as "untempered mortar". Consider the activities highlighted in the following passage from the book of Ezekiel 13:1-16 in that they describe some of the activities of parts of the church:

"And the Word of the Lord came unto me saying, "son of Adam, prophesy and say unto them that prophesy out of their own hearts, Hear ye the word of the Lord, Thus saith the Lord, Woe unto the foolish prophets that follow their

---

[46] Jeremiah 9:23-26 (Et Cepher 3rd Edition)

own spirit and have seen nothing. O Israel, your prophets are like the foxes in the deserts.

Ye have not gone up into the gaps, neither made up the hedge for the house of Israel to stand in the battle in the day of the Lord. They have seen vanity and lying divination, saying "the Lord says" and the Lord has not sent them, and they have made others to hope that they would confirm the word.

Have ye not seen a vain vision, and have ye not spoken a lying divination, whereas ye say, the Lord says it; albeit I have not spoken? Therefore, thus says the Lord, because ye have spoken vanity and seen lies, Therefore, behold, I am against you, says the Lord. And my hand shall be upon the prophets that see vanity and that divine lies; they shall not be in the assembly of my people, neither shall they be written in the writing of the house of Israel, neither shall they enter into the land of Israel.

And ye shall know that I am the Lord, because, even because they have seduced my people, saying, Peace and there was no peace; and one built up a wall and others daubed it with untempered mortar. Say unto them which daub it with untempered mortar, that it shall fall. There shall be an overflowing shower and ye, O great hailstones shall fall, and a stormy wind shall rend it. Lo, when the wall is fallen shall it not be said unto you, where is the daubing wherewith ye have daubed it?

Therefore, thus says, the Lord, I will even rend it with a stormy wind in my fury, and there shall be an overflowing shower in my anger, and great hailstones in my fury to consume it. So, will I break down the wall that ye have daubed with untempered mortar and bring it down to the ground, so that the foundation thereof shall be discovered, and it shall fall, and ye shall be consumed in the midst thereof:

and Ye shall know that I am the Lord. Thus I will accomplish my wrath upon the wall, and upon them that have daubed it with untempered mortar, and will say unto you, The wall is no more, neither they that daubed it; to wit, the prophets of Israel which prophesy concerning Jerusalem and which see visions of peace for her, and there is no peace says the Lord."[47]

The clear description of behaviors that characterize the "builders of the wall" also answers the question, "Who is it that has corrupted my vineyard?"[48] This outgrowth of actions based on misunderstood foundational teaching is truly what the passage in Ezekiel describes. These misunderstandings at foundational levels, especially knowledge and comprehension,

---

[47] Ezekiel 13:1-16 (Et Cepher 3rd Edition)
[48] Jacob 5:47 (The Book of Mormon, 1830)

led to poor, inaccurate evaluations. This is evident as the systems operating under these conditions have been unsustainable; errors at the knowledge and comprehension levels have caused faulty application.

Before getting farther into the details, I must acknowledge the undertones of my language that connote blame of specific groups of individuals for the current condition. No flesh is righteous in the sight of the Lord and all our righteousness are as filthy rags; we are all guilty.[49] As I will continually show, labels don't define groups, behavior does; a tree is known by its fruit. Our goal is to ultimately move to the Lord's side and yield the fruit of righteousness. (More on this later.)

Throughout the sojourn of the nation of Israel though, the nations that chose to come against them did it for different reasons. There are clear places in scripture that describe how the enemies of the Lord made plans to take the temple into possession along with the "holy things" for various reasons.

In 1 Maccabees Chapter 1, Antiochus is recorded as having defiled the temple of the Lord in his pursuit of the dominion of lands:

---

[49] Isaiah 64:6 (The Open Bible)

"And after that Antiochus had smitten Mitsrayim (Egypt), he returned again in the hundred forty and third year and went up against Israel and Jerusalem with a great multitude and entered proudly into the sanctuary and took away the golden altar and the menorah or light and all the vessels thereof. And the table of the showbread and pouring vessels and the vials and censers of gold, and the veil and the crown and the golden ornaments that were before the Temple, all which he pulled off. He took also the silver and the gold and the precious vessels: also, he took the hidden treasures which he found. And when he had taken all away, he went into his own land having made a great massacre and spoken very proudly. Therefore, there was a great mourning in Israel in every place where they were; so that the princes and elders mourned, the virgins and young men were made feeble and the beauty of women was changed. Every bridegroom took up lamentation and she that sat in the marriage chamber was in heaviness. The land also was moved for the inhabitants thereof, and all the house of Jacob was covered with confusion." (The New Oxford Annotated Apocrypha Third Edition, 1989)

Though the above account shows the wickedness of outsiders, earlier in the same passage is a description of the wickedness inside Israel because of a preference for the ways of the heathen:

"In those days went there out of Israel wicked men, who persuaded many, saying, let us go and cut a covenant with the heathen that are round about us; for since we departed from them, we have had much sorrow. So, this device pleased them well. Then certain of the people were so forward herein, that they went to the king, who gave them license to do after the ordinances of the heathen…"[50]

The "wall" that is built is that which is constructed to block out and defend against the ways of the Lord while keeping and protecting other ways. Whether from inside or outside, known or unknown, men have either not truly understood the Lord's ways or defiantly opposed them. At the destruction of Jericho Joshua says, *"Cursed of the Lord be the man who shall undertake to fortify this city of Jericho: he shall lay its foundations at the cost of his first-born, and set up its gates at the cost of his youngest."[51]* When this city was rebuilt it was written,

"Behold, an accursed man of Belial has risen to become a fowler's net to his people, and a cause of destruction to all his neighbors. And his brother arose and ruled in lies, both being instruments of violence. They have rebuilt this city and have <u>set it up for a wall and towers to make it a stronghold of ungodliness</u> in Israel, and a horror in Ephraim and in Judah. They have committed an abomination in the land,

---

[50] 1 Maccabees 1:11-13 (Et Cepher 3rd Edition)
[51] Joshua 6:26 (The Open Bible)

and a great blasphemy among the children of Jacob. They have shed blood like water upon the ramparts of the daughter of Zion and within the precincts of Jerusalem."[52]

Hidden in another account of the cause of captivity for the nation of Israel is a declaration of truth in that it pronounces woe on behaviors despite who commits them:

"Woe unto them that draw iniquity with cords of vanity, and sin as it were with a cart rope: that say, let him make speed and hasten his work that we may see it and let the counsel of the Holy One of Israel draw nigh and come that we may know it! Woe unto them that call evil good and good evil; that put darkness for light and light for darkness; that put bitter for sweet and sweet for bitter! Woe unto them that are wise in their own eyes, and prudent in their own sight! Woe unto them that are mighty to drink wine and men of strength to mingle strong drink, which justify the wicked for reward and take away the righteousness of the righteous from him! Therefore, as the fire devours the stubble, and the flame consumes the chaff, so their root shall be as rottenness and their blossom shall go up as dust because they have cast away the Torah of Yahuah Sabaoth and despised the word of the Holy One of Israel. Therefore, is the anger of Yahuah kindled against his people, and he has stretched forth his hand against them and has smitten

---

them: and the hills did tremble and their carcases were torn in the midst of the streets. For all this his anger is not turned away, but his hand is stretched out still."[53]

The necessity of separation from other nations is outlined in the description of the ways of the other nations described throughout scripture. This separation is very important because it helps to define the <u>true nature of the punishment of captivity</u>. Before Abraham's death, he blesses his sons and grandsons, admonishing them to keep the ways of the Lord. In it he says,

"Separate yourself from the nations and eat not with them and do not according to their works and become not their associate; for their works are unclean and all their ways are a pollution and an abomination and uncleanness. They offer sacrifices to the dead and they worship evil spirits, and they eat over the graves, and all their works are vanity and nothingness. They have no heart to understand and their eyes do not see what their works are and how they err in saying to a piece of wood, "You are my god," and to a stone, "You are my lord and you are my deliverer and they have no heart."[54]

---

53 Isaiah 5:18-25 (Et Cepher 3rd Edition)
54 Jubilees 22:16-18 (Et Cepher 3rd Edition)

In captivity, ignorance of the right way is multiplied. It is in this ignorance that ones' true desires can be revealed. This can also be a very vulnerable place as ignorance and wickedness plant seeds that can create desires that can alter identity. When our *true* identity is revealed, what do we do or how much are we willing to change, or do we choose an identity born in wickedness due

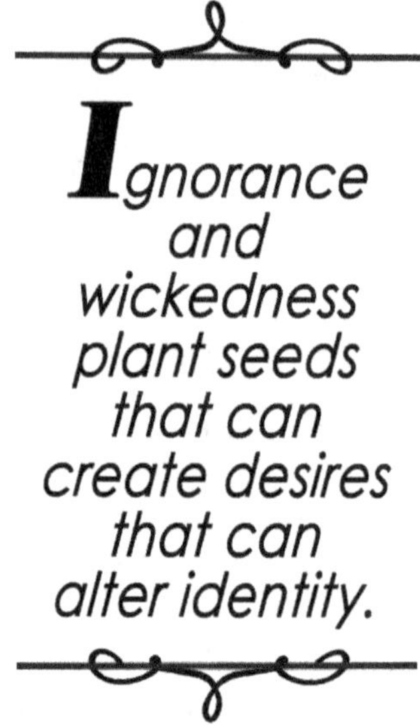

to ignorance? Levi is recorded as having described three ways that Israel becomes "trapped" or "caught" in its own wickedness:

1) Fornication,
2) The wealth of wickedness, and
3) The pollution of the sanctuary. (Charles R. H., p. 12)

"Whosoever escapes the first is caught in the second, and whoever saves himself from the second is caught in the third. The builders of the wall who have followed after 'precept' – 'precept' was a spouter of whom it is written, "They shall surely spout" – shall be caught in fornication twice by taking a second wife while the first is alive, whereas, the principle of creation is, male and female created he them..."[55]

---

[55] The Damascus Document (Vermes, 1962)

The wealth of wickedness describes that which is acquired through unjust gain. It can be something like offering a service that you have all but ensured you don't have to perform though it continues to enrich you. This describes only one form of unjust gain as many deceitful ways increase wealth. The pollution of the sanctuary was and is one of the most devastating consequences of captivity. Because the Lord fought for Israel, all activities in service to him and intercession for the people were crucial to experiencing the blessings of the covenant. However, due to disobedience, incest, and other sexual uncleanness, the priesthood was defiled.

In the passage quoted above, the word *spout* perfectly describes the preaching that often is built *line upon line and precept upon precept*[56]which reveals a faulty interpretation of the very scripture that supports the current *Christian way* of teaching. *"To whom shall he teach doctrine?"*[57]

"They also polluted their holy spirit and with a tongue of blasphemies they opened the mouth against the statutes of the covenant of God saying, "They are not established." But abominations they speak regarding them." (Charles R. H., p. 12)

---

[56] Isaiah 28:10 (The Open Bible)
[57] Isaiah 28:9 (The Open Bible)

The use of the *"wall"* to describe that which is built to guard against the ways of the Lord is just one way to frame it. Another quite effective way to frame the relationship of Israel to the Lord was marriage. The concept of *breaking wedlock* is synonymous with *taking the name in vain*. It describes a lack of faithfulness with intent to betray or abuse. It challenges the notion of fidelity to the one with whom vows were exchanged. Doing what one *must do* to keep things the way they want them despite their partner's wishes or needs is as if breaking wedlock; the other object of desire is one's own vanity. The word of the Lord to the prophet Ezekiel against Jerusalem includes this description specifically:

> *"Wherefore, O harlot, hear the word of the Lord: thus saith the Lord, because thy filthiness was poured out, and thy nakedness discovered through thy whoredoms with thy lovers, and with all the idols of thy abominations, and by the blood of thy children, which thou didst give unto them. Behold, therefore, I will gather all thy lovers with whom thou hast taken pleasure and all them that thou hast loved, with all them that thou hast hated; I will even gather them roundabout against thee, and will discover thy nakedness unto them, that they may see all thy nakedness. And I will judge thee as women that break wedlock and shed blood are judged, and I will give thee blood in fury and jealousy. And I will give thee into their hand, and they shall throw down thine eminent place and shall break down thy high places;*

they shall strip thee also of thy clothes and shall take thy fair jewels and leave thee naked and bare." [58]

Consider the conceptual nature of the transgressions listed up to this point; they offend the Father **despite who commits them**. Throughout the Psalms and other writings, accounts are given of the Lord's faithfulness to these descendants of Abraham despite the wandering nature of the Israelites and their perpetual choice to follow other ways. Consider this passage from the Damascus Document of the Dead Sea Scrolls:

"Listen now all you who know righteousness and consider the words of God; for he has a dispute will all flesh and will condemn all those who despise him. For when they were unfaithful and forsook him, he hid his face from Israel and his sanctuary and delivered them up to the sword. But remembering the covenant of the forefathers, he left a remnant to Israel and did not deliver it up to be destroyed. And in the age of wrath, three hundred and ninety years after he had given them into the hand of King Nebuchadnezzar of Babylon, He visited them and he caused a plant root to spring from Israel and Aaron to inherit his land and to prosper on the good things of his earth. And they perceived their iniquity and recognized that

---

[58] Ezekiel 16:35-39 (The Open Bible)

they were guilty men, yet for twenty years they were like blind men groping for the way.

And God observed their deeds, that they sought him with a whole heart, and he raised for them a teacher of righteousness to guide them in the way of his heart. And he made known to the latter generations that which God had done to the latter generation, the congregation of traitors, to those who departed from the way. This was the time of which it is written, "Like a stubborn heifer thus was Israel stubborn" (Hosea 4:16) when the scoffer arose who shed over Israel the waters of lies. He cause them to wander in a pathless wilderness, laying low the everlasting heights, abolishing the ways of righteousness and removing the boundary with which the forefathers had marked out their inheritance, that he might call down on them the curses of his covenant and deliver them up to the avenging sword of the Covenant. For they sought smooth things and preferred illusions and they watched for the breaks and chose the fair neck; and they justified the wicked and condemned the just, and they transgressed the covenant and violated the Precept. They banded together against the life of the righteous and loathed all who walked in perfection; they pursued them with the sword and exulted in the strife of the people. And the anger of God was kindled against their congregation so that he ravaged all their multitude; and their deeds were defilement before him. (Vermes, 1962)

Consider the behaviors shown and their relationship to some of the current behavior of those in the traditional religious sphere. We must continue to examine ourselves to see if we really *be in the faith.*

CHAPTER 5

Apocalypse

Why does this matter now? The proliferation of the church through the sacrifice of Christ brings damnation[59] to those **whose faith is falsehood**; as such, the error is very great! Consider the word of the Lord to Jeremiah,

"Hear now this, O foolish people, and without understanding; which have eyes and see not; which have ears and hear not. Fear ye not me? Saith the Lord. Will ye not tremble at my presence, which have placed the sand for the bound of the sea by a perpetual decree, that it cannot pass it: and though the waves thereof toss themselves, yet can they not prevail; though they roar, yet can they not pass over it? But this people hath a revolting and rebellious heart; they are revolted and gone. Neither say they in their heart, let us now fear the Lord our God that giveth rain, both the former and the latter, in his season: he reserveth unto us the appointed weeks of the harvest.

Your iniquities have turned away these things, and your sins have withholden good things from you. For among my people are found wicked men: they lay wait, as he that

---

setteth snares; they set a trap, they catch men. As a cage is full of birds, so are their houses full of deceit: therefore, they are become great and waxen rich. They are waxen fat, they shine yea, they overpass the deeds of the wicked: they judge not the fatherless, yet they prosper and the right of the needy do they not judge. Shall I not visit for these things? saith the Lord. Shall not my soul be avenged on such a nation as this? A wonderful and horrible thing is committed in the land; the prophets prophesy falsely, and the priests bear rule by their means and my people love to have it so: and what will ye do in the end thereof?"[60]

Again, the important question the Lord asks is, "*Shall I not visit for these things?*" The word of the Lord to the prophet was not always exclusively for Israel. The Lord did punish others for their ill-treatment of his people even when they (Israel) were being punished. The thirty-fifth chapter of Ezekiel records the Lord's decree against the people of Mount Seir because they went to war against Israel in a time of their (Israel's) punishment and attempted to possess the land.

"*Because you thought, "The two nations and the two lands shall be mine and we shall possess them," although the Lord was there. Assuredly, as I live, declares the Lord God, I will act with the same anger and passion that you*

---

[60] Jeremiah 5:21-31 (The Open Bible)

acted within your hatred of them. And I will make myself know through them when I judge you. You shall know that I the Lord have heard all the taunts you uttered against the hills of Israel: "They have been laid waste; they have been given to us as prey." And you spoke arrogantly against me and multiplied your words against me, and I heard it. Thus, saith the Lord God: When the whole earth rejoices, I will make you a desolation. As you rejoiced when the heritage of the House of Israel was laid waste, so will I treat you the hill country of Seir and the whole of Edom, all of it, shall be laid waste and they shall know that I am the Lord."[61]

Because the church has become worldwide, the *visitation* currently underway impacts the whole earth. Since the children of Israel have been scattered throughout the earth, foundations of deceit are being discovered and those that taunted and mistreated the Lord's people will have to answer for it! But, how many of the Lord's people are wicked? How many people are wicked in the name of the Lord?

---

[61] Ezekiel 35:10-15 (Tanakh: The Holy Scriptures, 1985)

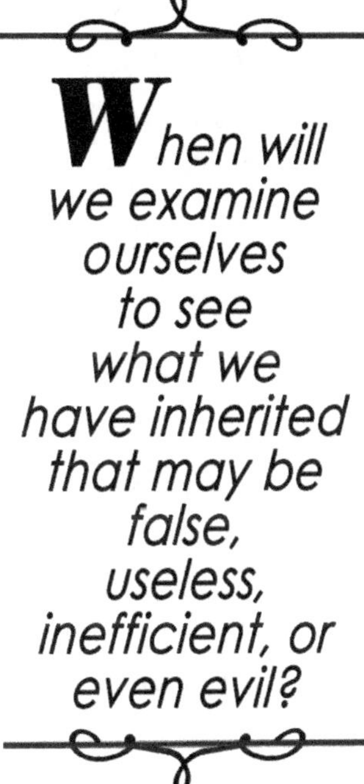

When will we examine ourselves to see what we have inherited that may be false, useless, inefficient, or even evil? If the day has come *again* that each man does what is right in his own eyes, what happens when the Lord shows us his ways and we knowingly reject them and him? The perpetual witnesses of the children of Israel demonstrate the power of his love in chastisement. The question I repeat is, "Do we love him back, truly?"

Do we still fear the Lord? Is our ignorance of him a hindrance to proper reverence? One of my other goals is to show how perfect the Lord is at keeping his word. His ways are perfect, and his plans are unfoilable. If we re-visit the words of Moses, we can see how consistent the Lord is at keeping his covenant though his people are consistently unfaithful to it. Chastisement is built into the covenant!

"If you fail to observe faithfully all the terms of this teaching (Torah) that are written in this book, to reverence this honored and awesome Name, the Lord your God, the Lord will inflict extraordinary plagues upon you and your offspring, strange and lasting plagues, malignant and chronic diseases. He will bring back upon you all the

sicknesses of Egypt that you dreaded so, and they shall cling to you. Moreover, the Lord will bring upon you all the other diseases and plagues that are not mentioned in this book of Teaching until you have been wiped out. You shall be left a scant few after having been as numerous as the stars in the skies, because you did not heed the command of the Lord your God. And as the Lord once delighted in making you prosperous and many, so will the Lord now delight in causing you to perish and in wiping you out; you shall be torn from the land that you are about to enter and possess.

The Lord will scatter you among all the peoples from one end of the earth to the other, and there you shall serve other gods, wood and stone, whom neither you nor your ancestors have experienced. Yet even among those nations you shall find no peace, nor shall your foot find a place to rest. The Lord will give you there an anguished heart and eyes that pine and a despondent spirit. The life you face shall be precarious; you shall be in terror, night and day, with no assurance of survival. In the morning you shall say, "If only it were evening!" and in the evening you shall say, "If only it were morning!" because of what your heart shall dread and your eyes shall see. The Lord will send you back to Egypt in galleys, by a route which I told you you should not see again. There you shall offer yourselves for sale to your enemies as male and female slaves, but none will buy."[62]

----

[62] Deuteronomy 28:58-68 (Tanakh: The Holy Scriptures, 1985)

If we contextualize slavery and its impacts narrowly and through the eyes of financial acquisition and the foundation of American wealth, we lose the reality that, for many of the people forcibly brought to the "New World", this captivity was a fulfillment of the Lord's word regarding the transgression of the covenant **and** his hand of extension to the other nations.

If we consider and look closely at how this was accomplished, the *ways* of those whose *vine is as Sodom* impacted more *people* than just Israel. The North Atlantic slave trade included many people from different lands. The fact is: we are all children of the Most High!

The captivity perpetuated during the Transatlantic Slave Trade was not without resistance. The method(s) used to "maintain order" represented psychological manipulation and an effort to *make slaves* captive in their minds. *The Willie Lynch Letter and the Making of Slave details* this process:

"While Rome used cords of wood as crosses for standing human bodies along its highways in great numbers, you are here using the tree and the rope on occasions. I caught the whiff of a dead slave hanging from a tree a couple of miles back. You are not only losing valuable stock by hangings, you are having uprisings, slaves are running away, your crops are sometimes left in the fields too long for maximum profit, you suffer occasional fires, and your animals are killed.

…My method is simple. Any member of your family or your overseer can use it. I have outlined a number of differences among the slaves and made the differences bigger. I use fear, distrust and envy for control.

The methods have worked on my modest plantation in the West Indies and it will work throughout the south. Take this simple little list of differences and think about them. On top of my list is "age" but it's there only because it starts with an "A." The second is COLOR or shade, there is intelligence, size, sex, size of plantations, the attitude of owners whether the slaves live in the valley, on a hill, East, West, North, South, have fine hair, coarse hair or is tall or short. Now that you have a list of differences, I shall give you an outline of action, but before that, I shall assure you that distrust is stronger than trust and envy stronger than adulation, respect or admiration.

The black slaves after receiving this indoctrination shall carry on and will become self-refueling and self-generating for hundreds of years, maybe thousands. Don't forget you must pitch the old black male vs. the young black male, and the young black male against the old black male. You must use the dark-skinned slaves vs. the light-skinned slaves. You must use the female vs. the male and the male vs. the female. You must have all your white servants and overseers distrust all blacks. It is necessary that your slaves trust and depend on us. Gentlemen, these are your keys to control. Use them. Have your wives and children use them, never miss an opportunity. If used intensely for one year, the slaves themselves will remain perpetually distrustful of each other." (Lynch, p. 8)

And there you have it: steal trust, kill unity, and destroy identity – the recipe of Satan. Because Christ told us what the enemy comes to do, we can properly reframe this process as a tool of correction from the Lord for his people, the goal of which is, to bring about *attrition of faith* that truly proves ones' faith to be true or false.

What about the others, those who suffered the same fate spoken of to this point in Willie Lynch's speech? These victims are testimonies to the Lord of the wickedness and brutality of *the people* and the grace of the Father. Which people? The *people* are the wicked who choose the ways described above and *walls* that promote unrighteousness. These *ways* do not indicate any specific group of people except that it classifies the behaviors of **any** people who oppose the Lord's ways.

At this point, the layers of intersection between the church, the remnant of Israel, and the United States of America become more pronounced and complex. The plan of Willie Lynch worked and was implemented with fidelity. In *The Mis-Education of the Negro*, Carter G. Woodson expounds on his observations of the plight of those that had then become known as Negroes despite many attempts to alter the name given to those who had essentially become a monolith in America.

The many identities of different tribes and or nations became blended into one. Captivity includes the removal of identity and aids in the achievement of extending chastisement from generation to generation as the promise of the Lord declared.

During this captivity, the education of the Negro after his mental enslavement was one rightfully deemed a "miseducation" of all things *"because it has been worked out in conformity to the needs of those who have enslaved and oppressed weaker peoples."[63]*

"No systematic effort toward change has been possible, for, taught the same economics, history, philosophy, literature and religion which have established the present code of morals, the Negro's mind has been brought under the control of his oppressor. The problem of holding the

---

[63] The Mis-Education of the Negro p. 2

Negro down, therefore, is easily solved. When you control a man's thinking you do not have to worry about his actions. You do not have to tell him not to stand here or go yonder. He will find his "proper place" and will stay in it. You do not need to send him to the back door. He will go without being told. In fact, if there is no back door, he will cut one for his special benefit. His education makes it necessary." (Woodson, p. 2)

The precarious life that would be experienced in the land of captivity was only punishment for the violating of the covenant as shown in the quote from Deuteronomy above. Again, this was a process of proving, separating and defining true identities. But what of the oppressors? Their deceit, vanity, and wickedness, all known to the Lord, were perpetuated throughout the system of education designed for people of color and continues to this day.

"The thought of the inferiority of the Negro is drilled into him in almost every class he enters and in almost every book he studies. If he happens to leave school after he masters the fundamentals, before he finishes high school or reaches college, he will naturally escape some of this bias and may recover in time to be of service to his people…The so-called school, then, becomes a questionable factor in the life of this despised people." (Woodson, p. 5)

Though this complete work was published in the early 1900s, many of the statements quoted are still true and can be observed in the poorer communities of the United States. Just as Willie Lynch proved on his own plantation, the system of mind control he taught in the American south, the breeding and breaking of people – making slaves, has continued for centuries. Though *morning is breaking,* because the bondage is of the mind, this mental wound of darkness and deceit must be exposed and replaced with truth, justice, and compassion with an attitude of reconciliation.

We must re-visit Willie Lynch's plan to see how to unravel the mental entanglements that are contrary to the Lord's ways. In addition to the fear, distrust, and envy used by Lynch's plan, long-range comprehensive economic planning was the ultimate goal of their processes. This started with the breaking of the African woman to produce the engine of their labor force – broken children. The plan was for these broken children to become forever *broken* as domesticated animals.

"For fear of the young males' life, she will psychologically train him to be mentally weak and dependent, but physically strong. Because she has become psychologically independent, she will train her female offspring to become psychologically independent. What have you got?

You've got the nigger women out front and the nigger man behind and scared. This is a perfect situation of sound sleep and economics. Before the breaking process, we had to be alertly on guard at all times.

Now we can sleep soundly, for out of frozen fear his woman stands guard for us. He cannot get past her early slave molding process. He is a good tool, now ready to be tied to the horse at a tender age. By the time a nigger boy reaches the age of sixteen, he is soundly broken in and ready for a long life of sound and efficient work and the reproduction of a unit of good labor force.

Continually through the breaking of uncivilized savage nigger, by throwing the nigger female savage into a frozen psychological state of independence, by killing off the protective male image, and by creating a submissive dependent mind of the nigger male slave, we have created an orbiting cycle that turns on its own axis forever, unless a phenomenon occurs and re-shifts the position of the male and female slaves. We show what we mean by example. Take the case of the two economic slave units and examine them closely."[64] (Lynch, p. 18)

The psychological manipulation articulated in the passage quoted above was considered crucial in the long-range planning of this "slave-making" system. While this plan was ultimately an economic one designed to perpetuate a system of mental and physical bondage, the intersection of the implementation of this plan through religion created its ultimate demise. Consider the following passage:

"Earlier we talked about the non-economic good of the horse and the nigger in their wild or natural state; we talked out the principle of breaking and tying them together for orderly production. Furthermore, we talked about paying particular attention to the female savage and her offspring for orderly future planning, then more recently we stated that, by reversing the positions of the male and female savages, we created an orbiting cycle that turns on its axis forever unless a phenomenon occurred and re-shifted the positions of the male and female savages.

Our experts warned us about the possibility of this phenomenon occurring, for they say that the mind

---

[64] The Willie Lynch Letter: The Breaking Process of the African Woman

had a strong drive to correct and re-correct itself over a period of time if I can touch some substantial original historical base, and they advised us that the best way to deal with the phenomenon is to shave off the brute's mental history and create a multiplicity of phenomena of illusions, so that each illusion will twirl in its own orbit, something similar to floating balls in a vacuum.

This creation of multiplicity of phenomena of illusions entails the principle of crossbreeding the nigger and the horse as we stated above, the purpose of which is to create a diversified division of labor thereby creating different levels of labor. The result of which is the severance of the points of original beginnings for each sphere illusion...

Crossbreeding niggers means taking so many drops of good white blood and putting them into as many nigger women as possible, varying the drops by the various tones that you want, and then letting them breed with each other until another cycle of color appears as you desire. What this means is this: put the niggers and the horse in a breeding pot, mix some asses and some good white blood and what do you get?

You got a multiplicity of colors of ass-backward, unusual niggers, running, tied to a backward ass long-headed mule, the one productive of itself, the other sterile. (The one constant, the other dying, we keep the nigger constant for we may replace the mules for another tool) both mule and nigger tied to each other, neither knowing where the other came from and neither productive for itself nor without each other." (Lynch, pp. 21-22)

The plan of division articulated above included deliberate and premeditated rape in addition to quite inhumane, brutality. *Creating the phenomena of illusions for a diversified division of labor* only stood to fail as they did not understand the *"substantial original historical base"* that the scriptures they used as tools connected the slaves to. Having come from Britain, much religious practice evolved from the warped Christianity that developed from the same vanity and envy that has afflicted men since Cain and Abel.

Despite the ungodly practices that it took to perpetuate such a system, it continued though many claimed to be followers of Christ and were avid churchgoers. There is an unmistakable correlation between the plan laid out by Willie Lynch and its execution in "Negro" life and the church's development in America. Because the "whites" had to make a conscious effort to degrade and demean the "negroes," it was impossible to separate the growth of the American church from its congregants. Blacks weren't allowed to worship or attend gatherings of any kind with whites for quite some time in America. Predominantly "African American" churches and denominations started and inevitably furthered the already thriving plan of division.

Again, this same procedure was deliberately implemented to limit or redirect the faith in the truth of the Gospel. What greater historical base can be referenced than the source of all creation? This double-mindedness, the ability to teach the gospel to manipulate and deceive while never intending to honestly *keep* the word of the Lord is precisely what Paul spoke of when he said, "*he that eateth and drinketh unworthily, eateth and drinketh damnation to himself, not discerning the Lord's body.*" [65]

The Willie Lynch letter alludes to experts having given warnings about the "possible interloping negatives" which reveals that the psychology behind this plan was developed beforehand and there was confidence in its efficacy. The plan had already been carried out in the British Isles and worked to support slave labor, which promised longevity for generations. This rampant division was the American church's inevitable result and it has changed the language of faith and flooded the market with its own brands and styles of division while portraying itself as *the* authority on spiritual things.

---

[65] 1 Cor. 11:29 (The Open Bible)

The Lord promised to *turn our glory into shame,* and he did just that. The doctrines and denominations that were developed using scripture seem to all be different methods of division and error at times. This division and error over centuries left the American *Negro* truly broken without an understanding of his true identity.

However, the scriptures in the Bible provided the *substantial original historical base*[66] to maintain a more honest doctrine and interpretation of scriptures, though patterned in the same error, through true faith and acceptance of the Holy Spirit. But in his broken and miseducated state, the cycle that was planned, for he who had become just a *Negro,* stuck. Carter G. Woodson laments in his reflections over what he observed in forty years of working with the *Negro* and *his* deficits with striking detail and honesty.

"Often the Negro businessman lacks common sense. The Negro in business, for example too easily becomes a social "lion." He sometimes plunges into leadership in local matters. He becomes popular in restricted circles, and mess of less magnetism grows jealous of his inroads. He learns how richer men of other races waste money. He builds a finer home than anybody else in the community, and in his social program, he

---

[66] I highlight this phrase of Willie Lynch to emphasize it as an example of the ignorance of the connection of some enslaved Africans to the God of Israel. It also reveals that they didn't believe their behaviors would be answered and weighed by God. It will be referred to repeatedly.

does not provide for many contacts with the very people upon whom he must depend for patronage. He has the finest car, the most expensive dress, the best summer home, and, so far, outdistances his competitors in society that they often set to work in child-like fashion to bring him down to their level…

While serving as the avenue of the oppressor's propaganda, the Negro church, although doing some good, has prevented the union of diverse elements and has kept the race too weak to overcome foes who have purposely taught Negroes how to quarrel and fight about trifles until their enemies can overcome them. This is the keynote to the control of the so-called inferior races by the self-styled superior. The one thinks and plans while the other in excited fashion seizes upon and destroys his brother with whom he should cooperate." (Woodson, pp. 20,23)

I have quoted a quite large portion of *The Willie Lynch Letter* and *The Mis-Education of the Negro* because, in spite of the disparity in their ages and how old they are, many of the conditions of the so-called *Negro* have not changed much and Willie Lynch's plan seems to still be working in many ways. I am disappointed when I read just what I have experienced today as a somewhat educated black man that has chosen to live with and attempt to uplift his own people. It is apparent to me that what we are waiting for is our own honest repentance or we'll stay stuck.

The primary point I have been trying to make thus far is that none of what I have mentioned, or others described, was an accident nor was it unseen by the Father. The apocalypse or uncovering that is taking place, even with this work, is just one facets of the release from mental bondage being made free by truth and acquiring the knowledge of it.

A major part of experiencing this freedom is acknowledging and confessing our true state of being while humbly realizing that the Father's love is beyond our ability to fathom or understand and we must honestly admit our faults and repent.

> *"And it shall come to pass, when all these things are come upon you, the blessing and the curse, which I have set before you, and you shall call them to mind among all the nations, which the Lord has driven you, and shall return unto the Lord and shall obey his voice according to all that I command you this day, you and your children, with all your heart and with all your soul; that then the Lord will turn your captivity and have compassion on you and will return and gather you from all the nations whither the Lord has scattered you. If any of yours be driven out unto the outmost parts of heaven, from thence will the Lord gather you: and the Lord will bring you into the land which your fathers*

possessed, and you shall possess it; and he will do you good and multiply you above your fathers. And the Lord will circumcise your heart, and the heart of your seed to love the Lord with all your heart and with all your soul that you may live. And the Lord will put all these curses upon your enemies, and on them that hate you, which persecuted you. And you shall return and obey the voice of the Lord and do all his commandments which I command you this day."[67]

Confession is good for the soul!

______

[67] Deuteronomy 30:1-8 (The Open Bible)

CHAPTER 6

True Repentance

Several displays of humility and repentance are modeled throughout scripture by many of those chosen by the Lord. 2 Chronicles 33 gives a summary of the reign of Manasseh, son of Hezekiah, which began ruling at the age of twelve. He is recorded as being wicked and evil in the sight of the Lord to the point that he led Judah and Jerusalem to do worse than the heathen nations. The same record in 2 Chronicles tells of Manasseh's prayer and humility before the Lord.

"O Lord, according to your great goodness you have promised repentance and forgiveness to those who have sinned against you, and in the multitude of your mercies you have appointed repentance for sinners, so that they may be saved. Therefore, you, O Lord, God of the righteous, have not appointed repentance for the righteous, for Abraham and Isaac and Jacob, who did not sin against you, but you have appointed repentance for me, who am a sinner. For the sins I have committed are more in number than the sand of the sea; my transgressions are multiplied, O Lord, they are multiplied! I am not worthy to look up and see the height of heaven because of the multitude of my iniquities. I am weighted down with many an iron fetter, so that I am

rejected because of my sins, and I have no relief; for I have provoked your wrath and have done what is evil in your sight, setting up abominations and multiplying offenses. And now I bend the knee of my heart, imploring you for your kindness. I have sinned, O Lord, I have sinned, and I acknowledge my transgressions. I earnestly implore you, forgive me, O Lord, forgive me! Do not destroy me with my transgressions! Do not be angry with me forever or store up evil for me; do not condemn me to the depths of the earth. For you, O Lord, are the God of all those who repent, and in me you will manifest your goodness; for, unworthy as I am, you will save me according to your great mercy, and I will praise you continually all the days of my life. For all the host of heaven sings your praise, and yours is the glory forever. Amen."[68]

Though Manasseh admits the greatness of his sins, his faith is revealed at the end of his prayer where he demonstrates knowledge that the Lord God is compassionate and full of mercy. As a son of Israel, he also would have known that the Lord promises never to take his love away from Israel though chastisement was also a part of the covenant. This prayer also represents repentance after being captured by an enemy as a result of the behaviors explicitly repented of. In other words, his repentance didn't end his consequences.

---

[68] Prayer of Manasseh (Et Cepher 3rd Edition, p. 1326)

We often celebrate Shadrach, Meshach, and Abednego for their declarations of faith before King Nebuchadnezzar in refusing to bow to an idol. It's worth noting here that I have recounted the Babylonian names of Hananiah, Mishael, and Azariah as they were renamed in Babylon, the place of their captivity. Likewise, the adoption of the last names of the slaveholders was only one part of the American tradition that renamed those in captivity.

This is significant because of Azariah's prayer, which, along with other Apocryphal works, was subsequently omitted from the canonized Bible, though it clearly expresses confession and praise, while adding context to the account of the same situation recorded in the book of Daniel. Had the remnant of Israel in captivity read the following prayer, it could have provided the *substantial original historical base* Willie Lynch warned about sooner. The omission didn't prove effective at preventing the connections to our substantial historical base but revealed the ignorance and malice of forethought present in the ways of the *good Christians* of the "New World."

"Blessed are you, O Lord, God of our ancestors, and worthy of praise and glorious is your name forever! For you are just in all you have done; all your works are true, and your ways are right, and all your judgments are true. You have executed true judgments in all you have brought upon us and upon Jerusalem, the holy city of our ancestors; by a true judgment you have brought all this upon us because of our sins. For we have sinned and broken your law in

turning away from you; in all matters we have sinned grievously. We have not obeyed your commandments, we have not kept them or done what you have commanded us for our own good. So, all that you have brought upon us, and all that you have done to us, you have done by a true judgment. You have handed us over to our enemies, lawless and hateful rebels, and to an unjust king, the most wicked in all the world. And now we cannot open our mouths; we, your servants who worship you, have become a shame and a reproach. For your name's sake do not give us up forever and do not annul your covenant. Do not withdraw your mercy from us, for the sake of Abraham your beloved and for the sake of your servant Isaac and for Israel your holy one, to whom you promised to multiply their descendants like the stars of heaven and like the sand on the shore of the sea. For we, O Lord, have become fewer than any other nation, and are brought low this day in all the world because of our sins. In our day we have no ruler, or prophet, or leader, no burnt offering, or sacrifice, or oblation, or incense, no place to make an offering before you to and to find mercy. Yet with a contrite heart and a humble spirit may we be accepted, as though it were with burnt offerings of rams and bulls, or with tens of thousands of fat lambs; such may our sacrifice be in your sight today, and may we unreservedly follow you, for no shame will come to those who trust in you. And now with all our heart we follow you; we fear you and

seek your presence. Do not put us to shame but deal with
us in your patience and in your abundant mercy."[69]

Just as the children of Israel transgress the covenant again and again, the Lord offers his chastisement and forgiveness after true repentance. The most awesome thing about the prayer above is that it took place in the furnace and the Lord not only sent an angel into the furnace with them but urged King Nebuchadnezzar to order their release. Upon their release, the king acknowledged that the God of Daniel and the three Hebrew boys was truly God. Quite often, the unbelief in the nations of captivity is changed by the presence of faith in those who do truly believe. Those who remain still in their unbelief suffer the consequences of that choice.

One of the more relevant examples of the nature of the *proving* process and its impact on Israel from the leadership down is in 2 Samuel 24. David, the man after God's own heart, causes the people to err through his choice as king though the scripture clearly states that the people of Israel incurred the anger of the Lord. As we have noted in several instances, the behavior of the people can cause chastisement at any time as the chosen people of God were to maintain a high standard of living in contrast to the other nations by way of their adherence to the covenant.

---

[69] Prayer of Azariah (The New Oxford Annotated Apocrypha Third Edition, 1989, p. 189)

"And again, the anger of the Lord was kindled against Israel, and he moved David against them to say, Go, number Israel and Judah. For the king said to Joab the captain of the host, which was with him, Go now through all the tribes of Israel, from Dan even to Beersheba, and number ye the people, that I may know the number of the people. And Joab said unto the king, Now the Lord thy God add unto the people, how many soever they be, a hundredfold, and that the eyes of my lord the king may see it: but why doth my lord the king delight in this thing? Notwithstanding the king's word prevailed against Joab, and against the captains of the host. And Joab and the captains of the host went out from the presence of the king, to number the people of Israel...

So, when they had gone through all the land, they came to Jerusalem at the end of nine months and twenty days. And Joab gave up the sum of the number of the people unto the king: and there were in Israel eight hundred thousand valiant men that drew the sword; and the men of Judah were five hundred thousand men. And David's heart smote him after that he had numbered the people. And David said unto the Lord, I have sinned greatly in that I have done and now, I beseech thee, O Lord, take away the iniquity of thy servant; for I have done very foolishly."[70]

---

[70] II Samuel 24:1-10 (The Open Bible)

I take care in going forward because I want to be clear that I am not in any way ascribing unrighteousness to the Lord but, rather supreme righteousness and justice. The covenant entered into by Israel throughout its generations *would be kept*[71] by the Lord even as it was an extension of the promise made to Abraham[72] and an answer to his (Abraham's) prayer for Jacob specifically.

> *"May El Elyon give you all the blessings wherewith he has blessed Noah and Adam; may they rest on the sacred head of your seed from generation to generation forever. And may he cleanse you from all unrighteousness and impurity, that you may be forgiven all the transgressions which you have committed ignorantly. And may he strengthen you and bless you. And may you inherit the whole earth. And may he renew his covenant with you. That you may be to him a nation for his inheritance for all the ages and that he may be to you and to your seed an Elohiym in truth and righteousness throughout all the days of the earth. And do you, my son Jacob, remember my words and observe that commandments of Abraham, your father..."[73]*

I also take great care as I go forward because the intersection of eternal providence, present-day activity and

---

[71] Genesis 28:15 (The Open Bible)
[72] Genesis 22:15-19 (The Open Bible)
[73] Jubilees 22:13-16 (Et Cepher 3rd Edition)

scriptural interpretation become much more complex. Even as I recount events chronicled in various scriptures, please take note of the conceptual nature of the point I am making; no one is exempt from the consequences of his or her actions. But the way the Lord has, through the covenant, allowed for *his rod and staff* to bring comfort and protection to his people speak only of his glory and his Name. He, by *proving* his people, knows if their love is sincere and if they will keep his covenant by their actions.

> **B**y proving His people, God exposes if the love of His people is sincere and if they will keep His covenant by their actions.

"Now these are the nations which the Lord left, to prove Israel by them, even as many of Israel as had not known all the wars of Canaan; only that the generations of the children of Israel might know, to teach them war, at the least such as before knew nothing thereof; namely, five lords of the Philistines, and all the Canaanites, and the Sidonians, and the Hivites that dwelt in mount Lebanon, from mount Baal-hermon unto the entering in of Hamath. And they were to prove Israel by them, to know whether they would hearken unto the

commandments of the Lord, which he commanded their fathers by the hand of Moses."[74]

Nothing is hidden from the Lord of all spirits. Because he controls all things and, whether *circumcised or uncircumcised,* those of us that have chosen to do his will have a responsibility to maintain a righteous judgment as to prepare the way for *his will to be done on earth as in heaven.* It is incumbent, then, on those who lead to understand and acknowledge error with humility and grace. When leaders acknowledge the error, change can occur; <u>it doesn't matter what the catalyst for that error was</u>.

It is incumbent on those who lead to understand and acknowledge error with humility and grace.

In this work, I endeavor to do the opposite of the pagan theology as was quoted above by Carter G. Woodson that has us looking just as was planned, like *backward ass long-headed mules.*[75] As stated previously, the *garden is corrupted* by error. While this error is largely due to ignorance, it (error) has created the necessary position of humility as we rely on truth to be revealed and change to occur.

While change can be good, the transitions necessary to perpetuate that change can be difficult. I believe sincerely that this **must** begin with the truthful confession and repentance

---

[74] Judges 3:1-4 (The Open Bible)
[75] The Willie Lynch Letter: Warning Possible Interloping Negatives

of ALL. As I am demonstrating throughout this work, the knowledge has been provided for us, but the Lord's will and timing are perfect; all things will be revealed.[76]

---

[76] Matthew 10:26

CHAPTER 7

Spiritually Gentrified

"Mankind is in a state of heedlessness having plunged into the desires of the world and fallen deep into slumber and there is not a single scholar of the Faith who is working to arouse it from this plight. Should anyone happen to awake, he will find himself incapable of following *The Path* because of his ignorance. When he questions the scholars about it, he finds them to be far removed from it and disposed instead towards their own whims." (Al-Ghazali I. , 2016, p. 84)

Earlier, I questioned how "Christian" doctrine accounted for those documents that had been recovered at Nag Hammadi and the Dead Sea Scrolls. Consider the following passage:

"This ignorance of the Father brought about error and fear. And error became dense like a fog, so no one was able to see. Because of this, error became strong. But she worked on her material substance vainly, because she did not know the

truth. She assumed a fashioned figure while she was preparing, in power and in beauty, the substitute for truth.

This, then, was not a humiliation for the illimitable, inconceivable one. For they were as nothing, this error and this forgetfulness and this figure of falsehood, whereas established truth is unchanging, unperturbed, and completely beautiful. For this reason, do not take error too seriously."[77]

Having been found in Egypt at Nag Hammadi in the mid-second century, why isn't it considered practicable scripture? The prophets Daniel and Baruch, just to name two, are recorded as being told to hide things that they had been shown and that they would be revealed *at the end*. While I uncover some of these things in this work, there is a wealth of knowledge that has been retained over successive generations that has been uncovered testifying to the greatness of the illimitable, inconceivable one.

To err is human, to forgive divine.[78] The Father has not only forgiven us, but he has told us of our error long before we ever committed it or realized it. This is where it starts to get tricky! Christ offered, through the gospel, a connection to the Father

---

[77] The Gospel of Truth (Barnstone & Meyer, 2003,2009) (Barnstone & Meyer, 2003,2009)

[78] Alexander Pope

and the ability to know the Father. What we have come to know is the Church.

Many times, in scripture, even as quoted above, the error and ignorance of those in leadership are what cause others to err. As such, the knowledge I offer from my station is designed to replace the ignorance of the Father with the truth. While Christ did this as well, the garden is still in need of repair due to a *veil of misunderstanding* and being void of the *love of the truth that they might be saved.*[79]

> *"Every man is brutish in his knowledge: every founder is confounded by the graven image, for his molten image is falsehood, and these is no breath in them. They are vanity, and the work of errors: in the time of their visitation they shall perish. The portion of Jacob is not like them: for he is the former of all things and Israel is the rod of his inheritance: The Lord of hosts is his name."*[80]

While this passage, if taken literally, speaks of idols in the physical sense, I submit that we have been led astray by error and ignorance to worship each other as idols. The *corrupted vineyard* has produced leaders that may be unwilling to acknowledge error due to vanity and pride. Honestly, *who can understand his errors?*[81] The growth of the Christian church has exponentially multiplied the number of "prophets" and or

---

[79] 2 Thessalonians 2:11-12 (The Open Bible)
[80] Jeremiah 10:14-16 (The Open Bible)
[81] Psalms 19:12 (The Open Bible)

leaders whose behaviors fit those prophesied about by many of the men of God.

> *"But what I do, that I will do, that I may cut off occasion from them which desire occasion; that wherein they glory, they may be found even as we. For such are false apostles, deceitful workers, transforming themselves into the apostles of Christ. And no marvel; for Satan himself is transformed into an angel of light. Therefore, it is not a great thing if his ministers also be transformed as the ministers of righteousness; whose end shall be according to their works."*[82]

Since the apostate church has infiltrated the process of spiritual growth with misguided information, new guidance must be scaffolded to accommodate independence and differentiation with the goal of truly walking in the ways of the Lord. To those to who it is given, we must be free to be tools of the Father rather than pawns of man.

With truth and the *right* knowledge, we can correct our course in an attempt to align the spiritual and the natural in ways that please the Lord. Truth must be of primary importance to the novice and specialist, teacher, and student.

Though the wall built with untempered mortar is to be destroyed, what happens to the *true* people of faith? In this

---

[82] 2 Corinthians 11:12-15 (The Open Bible)

generation of *increased learning* and technology, mass media has amplified the impact of *the individual* (ego) possibly extending its influence on our lives so much that it has been given a name - *influencers*. Just as the "builders of the wall" have, social media has exponentially perpetuated this effect at the choice of the user.

There are so many options, with varying frequency and intensity, for how to apply various bodies of knowledge without a real way to assess the quality of the information received. With these alternatives to traditional spiritual education, our influences can be altered severely by many extrinsic factors. Exposure can also impact what is sought insomuch as we can learn to choose what isn't good for us because of over-exposure. Nowadays there are algorithms that perpetuate this affect in many social media platforms.

It is extremely important, then, to know the Lord *truly* to avoid the worldly influences of the nation of our exile that have *become a snare* for us. This expansion of social media and the internet has provided an opportunity for people to choose their own truth. While the church's expansion added to error already being done, now, anyone can present anything and call it the truth. This has always been the case, of course, since not all sources are reputable despite the medium. This reminds me of a word from the Lord to Hosea:

"As they increased, so they sinned against me. Therefore, will I change their glory into shame. They eat up the sin of my people and set their heart on iniquity. And there shall

be like people like priest and I will punish them for their ways and reward them for their doings."[83]

There are so many ways that the increase of churches, ministries, and individuals that speak in the name of the Lord have become corrupted. Much of the same error that has happened due to ignorance has been imitated and calcified. As such, many of the behaviors that promote vanity, impatience, greediness, etc. are encouraged. In many ways, we've created *alternate idolatry* with ourselves as the centerpiece.

When that vanity and idolatry meet, self-worship ensues, and often demands are made on others to provide worship in obvious ways: ignore abuse, provide a loyalty that ignores the truth when we're shown in an *unfavorable* light, and dedicate one's time as if it belongs to us. All these things incur a response from the Lord and though I attribute consequences to his response, God is not mocked; we reap what we sow.[84]

---

[83] Hosea 4:7-9 (The Open Bible)
[84] Galatians 6:7 (The Open Bible)

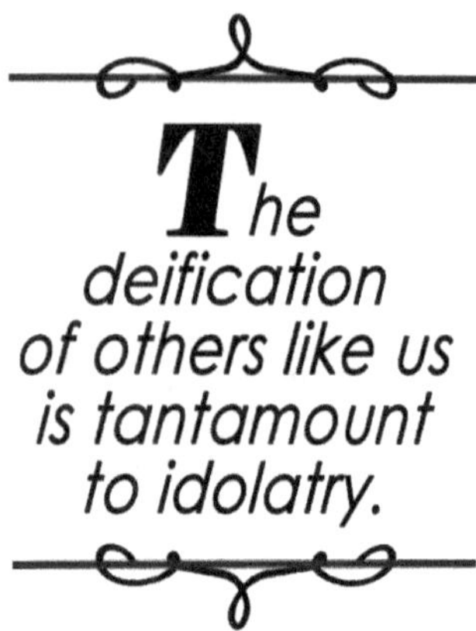

The deification of others like us is tantamount to idolatry. The subsequent worship that is given and even required in some cases, can obscure the truth of what is given and received. One way to ask for loyalty and commitment is to give another high status in *your* endeavor. Sometimes this is mutually beneficial, often it is not. Even Satan knew this when he tempted Christ, offering him the world if he worshipped him.

In this same way, it's interesting how religious circles throw the word *love* around. Like American culture, it seems love is defined quite narrowly and is used more as a tool of manipulation though we are taught "The Golden Rule," to love our neighbor as ourselves.

What does this really look like? What should it look like? Because all is vanity and flesh is so flawed, love is the most difficult thing for earthlings to do. As ever-learning beings, sometimes our knowledge, understanding and courage don't all mature at the same rate and we often make bad choices and fail repeatedly.

Only the Father's love is true and complete. ONLY the Father can see all of what and who we are and make an informed choice about us. He knows us intimately and accepts us with all of our flaws. This love is unmatched.

The *corruption that is in the world through lust*[85] has redefined love and used that lust against people. This lust is equivalent to covetousness in effect because it manifests as a strong craving for that which we don't have or don't need. Furthermore, it can be driven by being shown something that we wouldn't otherwise see.

But it is written that love never fails, and that God is love. So, what is this *thing* we are giving to each other that we call love? Over and over, it fails miserably! Our ignorance and vanity all but ensure the frailty of our *so-called* love. As such, most of our expressions of love are mingled with ignorance and selfishness. We must be careful how we attach ourselves to *loves* other than the love of the Father.

Remember: the love of money is the root of all evil and pride or love of self is a close second. Psalm 91: 14 describes the response of love from the Father to one who has *set his love on him*. The Hebrew word *chashaq* used in the psalm describes joining, clinging to, or delighting in another. The scripture shows the Lord's way of delighting in he who delights in him and seeks to know him.

Having been made in his image, we attempt to *chashaq* others through marriage and other unions and call it love. Because our Father is perfect and there is no respect of persons with him, he can join himself to us and make us better. When we join to each other there is potential, because of our

---

85 2 Peter 1: 4

many deficiencies, to cause more harm than good. Great caution should be exercised when joining another in any way!

Furthermore, unions and marriages that begin in debt and are weighted toward one side over the other can be like prisons. The "cat and mouse" game that we've been taught to play lacks honesty and practicality. It is truly a reflection of the amorality and polarization of society that prevents us from balance and achieving progress for all.

Often, it's these imbalances that have led to unwanted children, excessive debt, and extreme waste. In the context of love in some circles, it is more acceptable to talk about genitals, addiction, and extortion than faith and responsibility in truth.

Just as a coin has more than one side, so does the expression of love. Expressions that amplify love of fleshly activity can be more accurately defined as lustful. Whereas expressions that amplify truth and spiritual activity can better be defined as loving.

This is what makes sexual union very dangerous. In the garden, Adam and Eve didn't know they were naked until their shame and disobedience revealed it to them. The Father was already aware of them and saw no shame in *his* creation.

How do we get to the unity of faith without understanding of the truth? We seem to have become convinced that our will is commensurate with the Father's even though we pray *The Lord's Prayer* asking that *his* will be done on earth as it is in heaven.

But the media often contextualizes behaviors in ways that give observers things to identify with. Sometimes the identities we choose based on these constructs and the ones that are real and true don't match, in many cases, creating a *counterfeit consciousness.*

When this is done with malice of intent and forethought, the intention is robbery and the perpetuation of deceit and falsehood. This connects back to the *creation of a multiplicity of illusions* spoken of by Willie Lynch. The only problem now is that this isn't isolated to one population; anyone can live in the illusion they like except the truth is still true no matter what illusions are sought.

The multiplicity of illusions is perpetuated by and manipulated through television and social media. Because of its proliferation, one is almost compelled, if not forced, into participating just to maintain important contacts and or make a living. In many cases we create our own communities and become like zombies, blindly maintaining the illusions we've created.

The false sense of community we make for ourselves may create an even greater multiplicity of illusions all tied to our relationship with the Lord and each other. Sometimes the layers of things that we use to bring order to our lives create excessive clutter. This clutter can make it difficult to focus on those things that are true priorities.

Furthermore, a compartmentalized approach to life can prevent true wholeness. Taking each day, hour, and moment, as it comes while pursuing goals, can take away the anxiety of ambitious pursuits that require living in the future. Doesn't this situation reveal the conditions of the hearts of *all* of the people?

We have the ability to choose what or who we idolize and *worship* it or them openly and it's mostly acceptable. It can be difficult to find the line between abundant life and blindness when ambitious pursuits of wealth and status are considered a success for many. Service to the community and investing in other people often take a backseat.

If there was an understanding of what things are *really* true, it (social media and TV) could be an efficient tool in creating harmony. The problem is that the error prevents wise counsel and greed and vanity often turn, otherwise good things, bad. In many ways again, this leads to dissemination of information based on relevance to some and not others.

In America, this is a tyranny of the majority, especially because some Americans have, through deceit and cunning, created favorable situations for themselves while creating unfavorable cycles of poverty for others. Just as the ancient Israelites did, we overlay our will and confuse ourselves about who we are really following.

In this way, the churches have multiplied doctrine with *untempered mortar* as harlots, intermingling pagan elements with Hebrew faith and have become like the *sons of the sorceress and seed of the whore*.[86] Nowadays, the intermingling is that of American culture and church culture as opposed to a culture led by the actual ways of the Lord.

---

[86] Isaiah 57:3 (The Open Bible)

Often churchgoers don't seem to notice the correlations between national ways and church ways; the scriptures never mention a "first lady." Many churches, locally and nationally, mirror more of a democratic governmental structure where the focus is on one *head* that governs everyone else unless the governmental structure of the organization is strong enough for the people to control the pulpit.

The Bishops act as Gods sending preachers, pastors, and missionaries around to posts at *their* institutions. As stated by Carter G. Woodson, the spiritual needs of the people usually take a backseat to the man-made structures we've become accustomed to. We often treat prayer like money in America; we spend or pray for what we want sometimes without understanding what the Lord is trying to do with what we have. Part of our corruption lay in the fact that we've redefined things through our own eyes and built on it with the Lord's past interventions as our foundation.

Salvation, which was Christ's name in Hebrew defined, has been replaced with some representation of church experience and *not* experience walking with the Father. Even our language of outreach that used to include saved and unsaved has become more complex and people, often in need, are described as unchurched, re-churched, or de-churched. We have, hopefully inadvertently, left out the one from whom we heard the gospel message!

This reframing has created a *kingdom* that belongs to men without true respect for God's will. Consider God's response to David's desire to build a house for him:

> *"And it came to pass, when the king sat in his house, and the Lord had given him rest roundabout from all his enemies that the king said unto Nathan the prophet, See now, I dwell in a house of cedar, but the ark of God dwelleth within curtains. And Nathan said to the king, Go, do all that is in thine heart; for the Lord is with thee. And it came to pass that night, that the word of the Lord came unto Nathan, saying, Go and tell my servant David, Thus saith the Lord, Shalt thou build me a house for me to dwell in? Whereas, I have not dwelt in any house since the time that I brought up the children of Israel out of Egypt, even to this day, but have walked in a tent and in a tabernacle. In all the places wherein I have walked with all the children of Israel, spake I a word with any of the tribes of Israel, whom I commanded to feed my people Israel, saying, why build ye not me a house of cedar?"*[87]

The Lord's response to David was a very gentle reminder that, while the Father recognizes our love and appreciation for him, **we need him** not the other way around. When we forget this, we can let error creep in often due to zeal. Consider the story of when Christ made a whip and drove out

---

[87] 2 Samuel 7:1-7 (The Open Bible)

those who bought and sold in the second chapter of the gospel of John; he was upset about the *reprobate*[88] use of the temple.

> *"And he said unto the that sold doves, take these things hence; make not my Father's house a house of merchandise. And his disciples remembered that is was written, the zeal of this house hath eaten me up."*[89]

Even our emphasis on our ways of cataloguing and organizing scripture has caused us to focus on the letter and not the spirit. Canonicity exalts man's order and perspective above the Father's. But this error extends beyond canonicity. In many ways, we've trusted the commentaries and traditions of others without recognizing the contradictions in scripture. Christ challenged the religious leaders of his day about this as well.

> *"Then came to Jesus scribes and Pharisees, which were of Jerusalem, saying, why do thy disciples transgress the tradition of the elders? For they wash not their hands when they eat bread. But he answered and said unto them, why do ye also transgress the commandment of God by your tradition? For God commanded saying, honour thy father and mother; and, he that curseth his father or mother, let him die the death. But ye say, whosoever shall say to his*

---

[88] reprobate – unapproved; unprincipled; excluded as a measure of salvation
[89] Gospel of John 2:16-17 (Et Cepher 3rd Edition)

*father or his mother, it is a gift, by whatsoever thou mightest
be profited by me; and honour not his father or his mother,
he shall be free. Thus ye made the commandment of God of
none effect by your tradition. Ye hypocrites, well did Isaiah
prophesy of you saying, this people draweth nigh unto me
with their mouth, and honoreth me with their lips, but their
heart is far from me. But in vain they do worship me,
teaching for doctrines the commandments of men."*[90]

Too many in the church have become like the makers of
idols, more concerned about a loss of wealth than service to
the people of God. In the book of Acts chapter 19, the makers
of idols were enraged against Paul because the people chose to
do away with idolatry due to his preaching of the truth.
However, having convinced us of all of our great deficiencies
and making themselves the answer, some religious leaders *eat
up* the sin, pain, shame, and zeal of the people through the
people's ignorance. Often, they've been about the business of
perpetuating institutions as opposed to the relationships that
create them.

In truth, the relationships supersede the institutions as
they often work more efficiently without as many constraints.
There is much teaching and relationships have been made, but
many services in the church have become closer to
entertainment than religious or spiritual education. The

---

[90] Matthew 15:1-9 (The Open Bible)

messages that are often taught continue and even add error to the knowledge that has already been tainted.

For example, how many Latin songs, commentaries, and litanies omit the names of the Lord or many ways he was referred to? Even the word *hallelujah,* (in Hebrew and Latin form – alleluia), is omitted from Psalm 112 that opens, *"Praise the Lord,"* in the King James Version while in the Tanakh and other versions open with "Hallelujah." The significance of this omission is that, while it may be translated somewhat accurately, it replaces one of the names used for the Lord - *Yah*[91], with his title – Lord. This word is taught to be the highest praise in every language, but it isn't always clear why. We'll come back to this in a broader way a little later.

Titles and roles, in this way and others, help contribute to the multiplicity of illusions. How many words, titles, and rituals have been renamed for the purpose of deceit? If the bearers of truth behave dishonestly, darkness and falsehood are free to spread unchecked; ignorance can be taught as true knowledge.

We, because of ignorance, have not always been able to recognize our own wholeness or lack thereof because we have subconsciously rejected parts of God though we claim to be made in his image. Oddly enough, the requests or commandments of the Lord are for our benefit, yet we still reject them.

---

[91] Psalm 68:4 (Et Cepher 3rd Edition)

It is the vanity of man that allows him to forget his oneness with *all* while denying his connection to the whole. This is strengthened by ignorance of self, the goal of Willie Lynch's plan and the creation of a multiplicity of images attempts to ensure that this plan will continue forever.

> "By dividing life into separate halves and ordering the human being to cleave to one of these halves to the exclusion of the other the demiurgic power has caused humanity to do violence against the shadow side of the soul and has caused human beings to condemn themselves to a state of incompleteness and guilt." (Hoeller, pp. 34-35)

Loss of identity creates a vacuum that allows, even those that know your true identity, opportunities to alter and redefine it as *they* see fit often in hopes that you never find out. Ultimately, vanity can cause us to deny what is *actual* in pursuit of the hypothetical or ideal. It is actually more effective to chart a course that includes the transition from what *truly is* to what is desired.

> "Through the ages, the heart and mind have struggled with each other for dominion over the souls of men, and man has foolishly allowed his servants to become his masters." (Hall, 2017, p. Introduction)

The seemingly unperceived error of living in duplicity while teaching and creating multiplicity was that those perpetrating the error didn't foresee its impact on their own faith and families. This diversity of illusions and distorted use of language has broken down an ability to work effectively due to the disagreements about what is true versus what is an illusion.

Furthermore, in a market-driven, capitalist society, there can be an inability to sustain stability when forecasts and extrapolations can't be relied on based on a deficiency of knowing what is *actual*. If that which is illusory and temporary is defined as true, or even eternal, that which really is true and eternal becomes more difficult to recognize.

"Crossbreeding completed, for further severance from their original beginning, we must completely annihilate the mother tongue of both the new nigger and the new mule and institute a new language that involves the new life's work of both. You know language is a peculiar institution. It leads to the heart of a people.

Values are created and transported by communication through the body of the language. A total society has many interconnected value systems. All the values in the society have bridges of language to connect them for orderly working in the society. But for these language bridges, these many value systems would sharply clash and cause internal strife or civil war, the degree of the conflict being determined by the magnitude of the issues or relative opposing strength in whatever form." (Lynch, pp. 24-25)

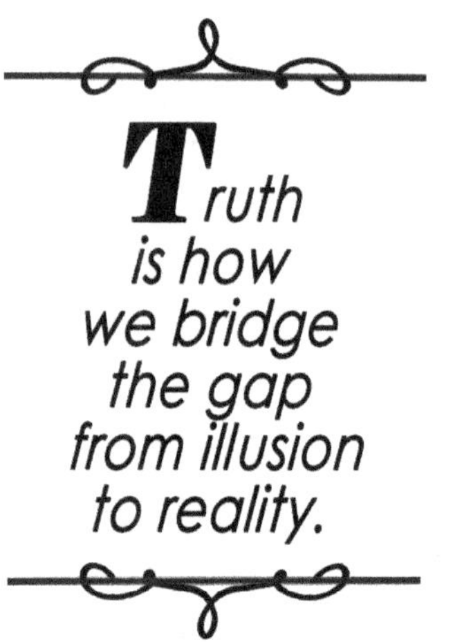

Our uses of language have evolved in a warped fashion to the degree that often, lust is identified as love, weddings are emphasized over marriages, "amount owed while in possession" is considered ownership, and access to information quickly and efficiently is regarded as knowledge. What do we *know* when we begin to engage things in their truth? Are we giving superficial attention to things because we have been afraid to engage ourselves *in spirit and in truth?* Truth is how we bridge the gap from illusion to reality.

We should consider Matthew 20: 27-28 and how we have rejected Christ's teaching about greatness. Our warped application of language coupled with our vanity has caused us to forget the levels of service that the ranks of leadership afford and demand.

Today's lack of emphasis on *true service* at the top of American government and by many leaders has caused many necessary things to be left undone. Some of our current leaders and those opposed to the ways of the Lord tend to see only that which is expedient and immediate, rejecting eternal wisdom, often condemning the behaviors of their enemies while condoning the behaviors of their comrades though the behaviors are the same.

The attempt to limit the eternal providence of the Father through a misunderstood chronology and vain pursuits of greatness often through the acquisition of material things, whatever they be, has led to mass confusion. Ignorance of true knowledge of the Father is much to blame – NOT the Father. In many ways, our choices to approve our ways above *his* ways reflect our attempt to limit God and reveal the depth of our own limitations.

So, then what of the illusions that are not sought but are prevalent due to beliefs that are shared though untrue? We've been weakened by an inability to embrace truth as American society and as believers in Christ. We have lost honest discourse to falsehood through etiquette, politeness, and deliberate deceit. Maturity and courage demand a true accounting of our time and efforts to grow. To improve, scrutiny and constructive criticism must occur; only then can we truly begin problem-solving.

We can integrate our communities synergistically with truth and knowledge of self. We do still need places of discovery and learning that operate for the good of the community and individuals. The key to maintaining progress is comparing apples to apples and trying to solve "real" problems. Trying to make a thumb be like a pinky toe isn't a problem to solve, but, in many ways, we approach issues with such a broad brush that we fail at the basic things and waste a lot of time.

Compulsion or to compel is to bring something about by force or to subdue. Being compelled into faith represents error that has increased bondage allowing us to deny the freedom that grace and truth provide. This compulsion through fear is contradictory to the very scriptures that we recite to encourage confidence. Spiritual or religious compulsion often include condemnation and dependency on something other than the Lord.

Incentives and severe consequences are subtle ways of compulsion. This is different than the freedom to choose that the Lord provides; he just lets us know the consequences of our disobedience up front and his grace and mercy are shown when he doesn't exact the full weight of consequences that he could because of his mercy and love.

Compulsion to faith in error often causes us to apply bandages in places where more serious interventions are needed. Dealing with root problems is complex and can take more time and effort which can expose places where *bandages* have failed already. When we don't actively and deliberately address the root causes of our deficiencies, we allow them to grow and become more difficult to deal with.

Here again, truth matters! At times, compulsion is a tool that perpetuates falsehood. When truth is known, this compulsion is less probable. Hell or the prospect of spending eternity there has been used as a tool of manipulation for church membership instead of the education that helps people to avoid the pitfalls and spiritual traps of our culture in a spiritually direct way.

Participation in church rituals while ignoring the problems that created the humility necessary to ask for help usually adds new problems to the old ones. The old issues then appear new adding confusion to disorientation helping to perpetuate old cycles. These cycles, without proper education, can become generational curses when this ignorance is passed down by behaviors that are taught and modeled from one generation to another.

Participation in church rituals while ignoring the problems that create the humility necessary to ask for help usually adds new problems to the old ones.

The expectations of others can also be used as tools of manipulation and compulsion when they are attached to hidden requirements, usually subjective in nature, that are often unrealistic or fickle. We can all use help to recognize our deficiencies, since we all have them, without deceit or manipulation. Honesty and meekness in our communication in appropriate situations can shine light on things we have trouble seeing and even hearing about.

However, setting traps for each other can be a tricky and ineffective way to influence someone to be what we think they should be. Christ warned woe to those who set snares and traps for others. In the King James Version of the Bible this sentiment is translated *offences*. The lying-in-wait for men and setting traps is not new behavior for the children of God. Jeremiah laments about this in Jeremiah chapter nine when he expressed not even wanting to live among them.

"Oh that I had in the wilderness a lodging place of wayfaring men; that I might leave my people and go from them! For they be all adulterers, an assembly of treacherous men. And they bend their tongues like their bow for lies but they are not valiant for the truth upon the earth; for they proceed from evil to evil, and they know not me, saith the Lord. Take ye heed every one of his neighbor and trust ye not in any brother: for every brother will utterly supplant, and every neighbor will walk with slanders. And they will deceive everyone his neighbor and will not speak the truth: they have taught their tongue to speak lies and weary themselves to commit iniquity. Thine habitation is in the midst of deceit; through deceit they refuse to know me, saith the Lord. Therefore, thus saith the Lord of hosts, *Behold, I will melt them and try them; for how shall I do for the daughter of my people? Their tongue is as an arrow shot out; it speaketh deceit: one speaketh peaceably to his neighbor with his mouth, but in heart he layeth his wait.*

> **Shall not I visit for these things**? *Saith the Lord: shall not my soul be avenged on such a nation as this?"*[92]

Community is built from families and while some organizations have been proxy for them (families), true connectedness and engagement characterizes healthy familial behavior. In families, not all members are the same but are connected to a *way* or *ways* that are largely shared even when new members are added through marriage. Sometimes these additions allow us to more objectively observe some of our ways and refine and evolve into more efficient, inclusive and intentional ways; change can be good!

---

[92] Jeremiah 9:2-9 (The Open Bible) bolded portions reflect author emphasis and are not the editions of the cited Publisher

CHAPTER 8

Turning the Corner

"For everything that is corruptible shall pass away and everything that dies shall depart and all the present time shall be forgotten. Nor shall there be any remembrance of the present time, which is defiled with evils. For that which runs now runs unto vanity and that which prospers shall quickly fall and be humiliated."[93]

If the Lord's people are destroyed for lack of knowledge, what is the value of much of our current knowledge? That which we seek to know for vanity's sake is empty and useless because we fail to learn to use it properly. However, that which edifies and builds up truth qualifies as the knowledge that has great value though we can use that which is undesirable to build up truth too. Even manure can nourish the beauty of fruit and flower. In this way, guidance and nurture are necessary to "grow strong plants."

With improper guidance, these plants can grow up and become bent out of shape. They may be able to bear fruit, but with proper framing and supports, more growth is possible. As we go forward, it is my goal to untangle that which nourishes

---

93 2 Baruch 44:8-10 (Et Cepher 3rd Edition)

because it's healthy from that which strengthens though intended to be harmful.

As stated before, *those that lead us cause us to err*, though not with malice in many cases. This can be good as living with the added weight of those who, in an effort to help you, hold you down actually also builds strength from the increased resistance. The problem is that those who hold you down only acknowledge your strength when you forcibly prevent them from holding you down. They often didn't realize that respect and submission made you stay down, not their force. Since many of us were truly submitted to the Lord anyway, we broke from those entanglements of error and deceit still in need of the community that church and other institutions were intended to provide.

The spiritually effective *counter* to an approach of condemnation and degradation is the perpetuation of true edification through knowledge and acknowledgement of our individual connections to that which is greater. Our knowledge base must grow to include those things that were deliberately left out to keep us from connecting to the Father of ALL – our true *significant historical base*.

But, how do you acknowledge truth except by the spirit of truth? Without the spirit of truth, the focus is unavoidably placed *on the letter* which killeth.[94] It cannot be understated the value of truly being present. Going through motions that lack authenticity is unsustainable; this often is the result of doing activities without a proper understanding of their purposes and consequences which can lead to unwanted mistakes.

The attachment of rituals and activities dictated by a calendar provides great planning and organization but cannot engage the hearts and minds of the participants without the truth of their intent. The imitation that the Christian religious calendar provides is the opportunity for us to reframe the knowledge they (Christians) have chosen and act on it, solidifying traditions that are often

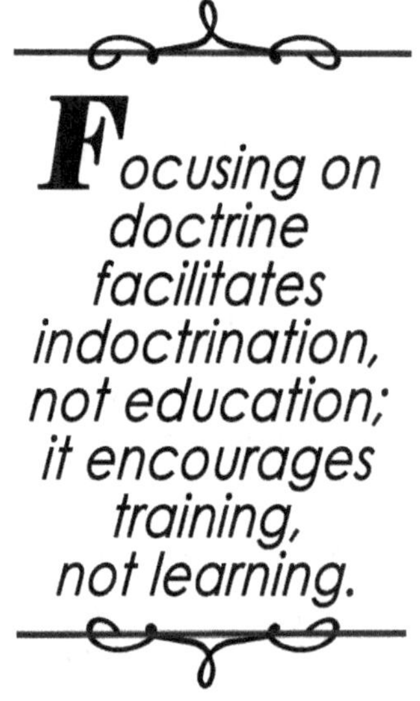

disconnected from their purposes and that don't truly reflect what they are designed to recognize but are fully enmeshed in the doctrine.

Focusing on this doctrine facilitates indoctrination, not education; it encourages training not learning. Learning accelerates and perfects training. Spiritual teaching must be deliberate, honest, and precise; it must have a "godly spiritual source". It can be beneficial to find helpful spiritual principles

---

[94] 2 Corinthians 3:6 (The Open Bible)

in that which is designed to destroy; knowledge of self can maximize learning of these principles. In order to truly turn the corner, we need to better deal with one of our common deficiencies – the diseases of the heart.

> "To learn this form of medicine, (treating the illnesses of hearts, it is incumbent upon all men of sense, since there is not a single heart which is free of diseases which, were they to be neglected, would redouble in strength leading to disorders still more frequent and powerful." (Al-Ghazali I. , 2016, p. 5)

If the heart or ignorance perpetuates sin, then they are or can be the enemy of the sinner, which we all are (sinners). This strengthens the notion that the focus should not be on arbitrary rules but on ways that promote a healthy heart. It is necessary, then, to juxtapose behaviors and states of mind.

What do we pursue? Is it natural or spiritual? Are our pursuits balanced with the Father's will? How do we gauge that? I believe balance is more circular than linear. This is evident as a truer explanation of sin is distance from the mark, as in darts.

Purpose and process can become confused when religious practice obscures the goal. Often, time and place are the unknowns in the pursuit of goals. A strong spiritual foundation can weather the storms of life and growth; this begins at home.

Spiritual independence is necessary as maturity and growth are measured by the Father. The ability to self-assess and commune with him is key to truly achieving balance and maturity throughout the changes that life brings

"Commit thy works unto the Lord and thy thoughts shall be established."[95]

Trying to exchange our sight for his can't occur without His mind. If we think like him, we can learn to perceive as he does. In this way, we must stay focused on him as he can see all. Practicing this builds trust. We, in some cases, have given this relationship to the church despite the "tearing of the veil."

Too often, the pursuit of what we want has outweighed the pursuit of what we need. In some ways, knowledge of self is fragmented in ways that have created a vacuum. Self-interest and true desires can be revealed as we seek to fill that vacuum with what we feel or think we need.

We don't often need what we want. Our limited vision prevents us from seeing all that we may be asking for. Furthermore, our contentment is often challenged by the idea that we deserve more than we already have. Humility allows us to appreciate what we have while attempting to purify our desires.

---

[95] Proverbs 16:3 (The Open Bible)

To heal a wound thoroughly, it must be exposed; then you can truly see the damage and apply the necessary tools. Acknowledgement of appropriate behaviors coupled with an effort to apply tools of correction can lead to healthier habits and thoughts. Because where there are many laws, there is much lawlessness, there is always room to criticize someone's behavior according to some scripture especially given that the seasons of life and growth include mistakes.

An approach using condemnation because of the transgressions of a particular precept is ineffective because it only addresses the symptoms and not the root causes of illness which are usually heart related. We must stop condemning the ignorant and start teaching with sensitivity and grace with a focus on true communication with the intention of doing the will of the Father rather than operating on experience, personal assessment, or dogma.

Rather than focusing on esoteric mysteries, we should use our spiritual energies to combat the diseases of the heart. Its wickedness and illnesses vary, but self-awareness and truth can help us to guide our actions in a way that can help to compensate for our deficiencies. Because *what things look like* and *what they are* can be different, we can benefit by approaching situations with care.

If we believe we have a better way, it is helpful to know why and be able to accept the possible disagreement of another. If we believe someone else's way is flawed, we may need ways to describe our perception of the flaw(s) and suggest remedies that are objective. However, the wholesale condemnation of differences, especially passive-aggressively, only serves vanity if no one is bettered by the exchange. There can also be fundamental disagreement due to spiritual perspectives that probably should end with agreeing to disagree.

Sometimes, those who know things that we may need can be so condescending that their attempts to help aren't received well. Sometimes, what we need may hurt so much that we avoid it; pursuing it can expose other areas we've tried to avoid that need to be addressed as well. Often the task appears so daunting, we choose to tread water where we are rather than plan a way out. Often, the way out involves confronting what we've avoided.

There must exist a re-visitation of what knowledge is fundamental to teaching higher-order "spiritual concepts," some of which should not be taught *en masse*. Weakness due to the wasteful expenditure of spiritual energy can be corrected if that energy is redirected. Only due to the narrowing of spiritual perspectives from teaching "in error" must we do this; the fear of the Lord is taught by the precept of men.[96] Because the foundation of all things is spiritual, all lasting natural and material things are functional or righteous as the Lord of ALL spirits says.

But how do you define righteousness, then, or distinguish between what's truly right or wrong? Only the

---

[96] Isaiah 29:13 (The Open Bible)

creator can assess whether something is working as designed. The Lord's choice or what's right is a much better measure of "right" than man's judgment. We tend to condone what we allow, which can be flawed judgment as we often allow things that we know can become detrimental.

Sometimes we don't condone things but still allow them. For example, I don't condone dogs in the bed, but I've allowed it to some degree ever since I had dogs of my own. Often this is because we don't live in a vacuum and life is quite fragile and complex. It stands to reason that there are many ways to define righteousness that are all accurate depending on vantage point and perspective.

The apple tree is not more righteous than the oak because it appears to bear no fruit that humans commonly eat. Hence, the Lord's definition, application, and identification of righteousness are largely unknown and different than ours because he knows what he planted and knows what to expect from each.

Righteousness is both a means to an end and a resting end at the same time. Because of the consistency of change, righteousness is not static. It is extremely important to use "right" measures in all situations making connection to the Father of great necessity.

Having lost some of the practicable nature of some of our symbolism and religious practice, we have promoted the vacuum that was filled with ignorance. Reclaiming the fundamental truth of these things will expose and help us to remove deceit and corruption and live more honestly.

Have we learned to separate the person from the purpose so well that we don't really see each other? Have we become so vain and idolatrous that we have lost sight of the harmony things were created to live with?

Action occurs on many levels of existence; therefore, not all actions can be observed. Knowledge of some perpetual action may prevent acknowledgment of other unrecognized actions. It's possible to disregard many of the sun's impacts on earth due to limited perspective.

Similarly, the process by which sound waves are interpreted in recognizable patterns by the brain cannot be seen but cannot be denied. Therefore, a lack of knowledge of all variables makes people interdependent while completely dependent on activity that is unseen both inside and outside of the body.

As such, we give our analyses too much credit. The humility to acknowledge our error in the assessment of another is best when God-given. The better thing to analyze is why we're assessing another person in the first place. People are complex; consequently, there are many unknown variables. When analyzing and assessing others, we must remain objective and practical. It is illogical to base an assessment of a plumber on his favorite football team. Similarly, it is not prudent to assess the character of a person by what we see, especially without considering so many of the variables.

Variables can change an entire equation! Because growth and change are constant, more grace can be extended to others in our interactions. Impatience and hard-heartedness can be the enemies of grace on the giving and receiving ends. A willingness to smooth tension through understanding and honesty can build the capacity to weather transitions and situations that require collaboration.

The only reason we can say, "If it looks like a duck and quacks like a duck, it's probably a duck," is because we are unaware of other animals that share those characteristics. We must remember that shared characteristics don't always indicate sameness. Granny Smith apples have much in common with Fuji apples concerning characteristics, but the taste is very different; both are still good apples.

Furthermore, visiting Alaska wouldn't give an accurate perspective of the entire United States though a part of it. Visiting Lake Michigan in August is a much different experience than visiting the same location in January. My point is that we can improve honesty by being present.

Spiritual education then, must not exploit emotion and ecstasy though the Holy Spirit stirs both as we get close to the Father. We aren't supposed to exploit the light for darkness' sake. True light drives out darkness giving darkness value only as it clarifies its own boundaries.

Light and darkness each work synergistically to accomplish the will of that which is greater than both. The light that guides our steps as we move about with faith changes from darkness to light or from night to day; we often see things that were there all along.

As knowledge of the "right way" impacts what we do, our judgment reflects this change becoming captive no longer. This is the strength of the knowledge Christ offered; one of his declarations of intent listed in the book of Isaiah was to give liberty to the captives. This captivity can be experienced in the cycles of sin, especially as we truly understand what sin is.

Freedom comes with being free of the ignorance of our place in the cycle and conscious effort to live in our new light. The question becomes: can that which was born in the darkness survive the light? Won't the light reveal the truth of what was born in darkness? If it survives, there may be light in it; if it dies, it was possibly only useful in the darkness.

An effective way to kill a plant can be to starve it of nutrients and deliberately withhold that which would make the plant thrive. How much damage has been done by the malicious withholding of the light of spiritual truth? In some ways, recorded history is more about another's assessment of relevance; relevance can be a subjective assessment.

A collection of chronological events cannot be divorced from the perspective of the collector, thereby creating *his*tory. This calls into question the entire idea of systematic theology which, according to Grudem,

"…involves collecting and understanding all the *relevant* passages in the Bible on various topics and their summarizing their teachings clearly so that we know what to believe about each topic." (Grudem, p. 17)

If that which is true is deemed irrelevant, those for whom the knowledge was meant may be unaware of it due to its omission. This calls into question the deliberate omission, for some, of the Apocryphal works' inclusion in the bible. It also raises the question of whether Christian doctrine has evolved since the uncovering of documents found in the Dead Sea Scrolls and at Nag Hammadi to name just two sources. Many of these documents help to contextualize other scriptures in ways that promote the unity and oneness of the gospel and, in ways, correct and clarify expectations.

CHAPTER 9

Neo Pistis Sophia

The real question and idea to explore in detail is what we have lost in the context of how to get it back? We have lost so much, and many things have been shaken and removed from us - some for good and some for bad. We cannot deem things known because they have been named or memorized. We must certainly not deem things that are *seen* as known or understood; that which we "know" is that which alters how we think and feel while influencing what we do.

However, not just the acquisition of knowledge is important but how and why we're trying to learn or acquire it. How often have college students changed majors after realizing that they didn't *know* what they *learned* about how to fulfil their own desires!

Knowledge is greater than the sum of facts and figures gathered and catalogued over time. True *gnosis* or *yadah*, to use a Hebrew word, is that which can be functional or useful. As such, the greater one's functional knowledge base is, the more productive one can be. Controlling knowledge through envy, mistrust, deceit, and a multiplicity of illusions, all of Willie Lynch's self-acknowledged tools, was not possible without careful use and manipulation of language.

Language and context can be a strong tool in understanding the specific usage of a word and a great tool in reading a situation. Altering and or removing contextual factors can promote misunderstandings that change meanings and modes of application.

As I continue to untangle some of the knots that have tied up our knowledge and understanding, I will continue to employ *truths* gathered from diverse sources as I attempt to show the degree to which much of our current practice needs to be adjusted.

A closer look at *knowledge* from educators' standpoint will help in our ability to analyze our current practices more closely.

"Knowledge, as defined here, includes those behaviors and test situations which emphasize the remembering, either by recognition or recall, of ideas, material, or phenomena. The behavior expected of a student in the recall situation is very similar to the behavior he was expected to have during the original learning situation. In the learning situation, the student is expected to store in his mind certain information, and the behavior expected later is the remembering of this information. Although some alterations may be expected in the material to be remembered, this is a relatively minor part of the knowledge behavior or test. The process of relating and judging is also involved to the extent that the student is expected to answer questions or problems which are posed in a different form in the test situation than in the original learning situation.

Each subject field has a body of techniques, criteria, classifications, and forms which are used to discover specifics as well as to deal with them once they are discovered. These differ from the specifics in that they from the connecting links between specifics, the operations necessary to establish or deal with specifics, and the criteria by which specifics are judged and evaluated. It must be made clear that this class of behaviors is only a very limited one as used here. It does not involve actual use of the ways and means so much as it does a knowledge of their existence and possible use.

1. Knowledge of Convention
2. Knowledge of Trends and Sequences
3. Knowledge of Classifications and Categories
4. Knowledge of Criteria
5. Knowledge of Methodology
6. **Knowledge of the Universals and Abstractions in a Field**

a) Knowledge of the major ideas, schemes, and patterns by which phenomena and ideas are organized

b) Knowledge of Principles and Generalizations

c) Knowledge of Theories and Structures" (Bloom, pp. 62-67)

Many of the ways that laymen are offended by the church can be summed up by the apparent attempt to continue with *business as usual.* If we know better, why haven't we done better? I quoted Carter G. Woodson at length earlier and he gave many solutions in his constructive analysis, yet we haven't implemented them with fidelity. Our success in truly *turning the corner* hinges on our ability to put what we learn into practice *in spirit and in truth.*

I will begin adding to basic knowledge with a closer look at defining the language we use before reframing it. Faith is a foundational word in spiritual language. Its most common Christian definition is found in Hebrews Chapter 11 verse one. However, the *"things"* hoped for has been redefined in a material sense though the definition of faith really hearkens back to the Hebrew understanding.

Grudem says that scripture puts faith with repentance "as different aspects of the one act of coming to Christ for salvation." (Grudem, p. 310) In his doctrine, "the heart attitudes of repentance and faith <u>only begin at conversion.</u>"

(Grudem, p. 313) This notion is surprising in light of even New Testament, canonized scripture. Grudem's approach treats faith as a New Testament construct, again ignoring the foundational aspects of Hebrew scripture. Paul even articulates a process of growth and maturity in knowledge of the Father that grows *from faith to faith* in righteousness.

> *"For I am not ashamed of the gospel of Christ: for is the power of God unto salvation to everyone that believeth, to the Jew first and also to the Greek. For therein is the righteousness of God revealed from faith to faith: as it is written, The just shall live by faith. For the wrath of God is revealed from heaven against all ungodliness and unrighteousness of men, who hold the truth in unrighteousness; because that which may be known of God is manifest in them. For God has showed it to them."*[97]

The common Hebrew word for faith comes from the word *emuwn* meaning that which is established. *Emuwnah* or *Emunah,* equal in Aramaic, also means faith and is used forty-nine times throughout Old Testament scripture. It literally means *firmness*; this is synonymous with *that which is established*, the definition of *emuwn*.

Our faith is what connects us to *The One* we cannot see, but we hope in his truth. Our acknowledgment of his interventions in our lives is the *evidence* that we can't see or

---

[97] Romans 1: 16-19 (The Open Bible)

explain though we know it to be true. Often this is what non-believers attack with non-spiritual, scientific knowledge. Often the goal is to disprove the truth of the Father's love for us or our ability to believe or rely on it.

The wisdom of faith is a more efficient study than theology, the study of God. What value is it to work to explain the incomprehensible? I believe there is more value in trying to understand that which is within our grasp. Faith differs from religion in that religion is rigid and true faith is fluid. Religion can be so fixed on itself that its means take precedence over its ends.

As such, a question of what we believe and why believe it is essential. An ability to question our traditions and habits helps the authenticity in our practice of faith. This can be unsettling if our perceptions are based in untruth. This is why I've titled this chapter "New Wisdom of Faith" in Greek.

Codifying the behaviors of a living, unlimited spirit is misguided. Often the process of building a working knowledge of The Providence cements the relationship that religion misses. Structures created to assume those individual spiritual responsibilities can only do so much.

A true analysis of our faith eventually leads us to examine what we believe about ourselves. Where do our core beliefs come from? What are the facts behind what we believe to be true? Does our belief system have a strong foundation? Are we strong enough to really look closely at our lives from this vantage point? Living comes with being honest with ourselves.

A framework of faith is important because of the way the mind works. The serpent knew this in the garden with Eve when he approached her with subtlety. Hidden behind the threat of exile and disobedience was the fruit of the seed that the serpent planted. This fruit is the idea that we are as "gods" because we have knowledge of good and evil.

This idea of balancing good and evil as a binary construct reveals the limits of the mind due to framework. The Father, The Providence maintains all things within every framework; we have no framework that "he" can fit into. Our issue is that knowledge and ability to trust the Providence must be learned over time.

Driven by faith, we can balance our efforts with the fact that the creator has truly provided all things. For this reason, I have adopted The Providence as one of my primary descriptions of the Father. It infers no gender and doesn't hearken to any religion widely practiced today. The Providence gives without the recipient understanding the giver's source(s).

True balance lies in an ability to understand our reliance on what we're given instead of what we give. Furthermore, what we create cannot be our source since we too have a source outside of our control. Our greatest waste of time and resources comes from our over consumption of our own creation(s). This is the epitome of idolatry.

CHAPTER 10

Me vs. My Image

"From the double life every American Negro must live, as a Negro and as an American, as swept on by the current of the nineteenth while yet struggling in the eddies[98] of the fifteenth century, from this must arise a painful self-consciousness, an almost morbid sense of personality and a moral hesitancy which is fatal to self-confidence…Such a double life, with double thoughts, double duties, and double social classes must give rise to double words and double ideals, and tempt the mind to pretense or to revolt, to hypocrisy or to radicalism." (Dubois, p. 122)

Though I quoted W. E. B. Dubois in chapter three using the exact same quote as I begin this chapter, it bears repeating in the context of truly growing and realizing our deficiencies collectively and individually. Knowing the Lord isn't enough! Often, we need help seeing ourselves truly to begin, or

---

[98] eddy – a small whirlpool

continue, on a path toward him. Knowing ourselves deeply helps us to see our true values and deficiencies. We can then choose how to proceed with or without help.

Submission to the Father allows us to attain the level of humility that promotes healing. As we acknowledge our absolute reliance on the Father, we can focus our efforts on him which actually improves us so much that we become refined.

As long as men grapple with the flesh, there needs to be guidance that allows us to win the battle against the vanity of flesh. The insidious nature of vanity often prevents us from recognizing the depth of our bondage to ourselves.

Sometimes we're taught to put so much emphasis on how we want others to see us that we neglect knowing ourselves truly. This may be a perceived necessity to operate in the workplace, home and so on! Our perceptions of how others see us still comes through the filter of our own experiences.

It takes an influential love that can help us that only comes from the Father to endure our own cleansing. The spiritual filth that we acquire can be overwhelming. Over time we develop expectations based on repeated patterns of experiences that can shape our perspective for good or bad.

Breaking the patterns of expectation that sometimes drive action is difficult alone. When we don't see each other due to the vanity of our ways, we tend to isolate. Most of us are very filthy and believe others can see what we actually feel, though many times they cannot.

True godliness includes maintenance of right intentions while knowing our own good and evil. The only reason we possess knowledge of good and evil in the first place is due to disobedience. The Father knew what Adam and Eve would choose though he told them not to.

Ironically, the fall from the garden is what contextualizes salvation and reveals the Father's love for us as parental love and correction that is unconditional. This highlights the necessity for community as we all need to experience the friction that refines us though we usually cause the problems.

In this way, institutions that aim to merge service with practical life tasks will help to propel us into greater unity. One of the things I've expounded on consistently is how the church in many cases reflects the prophecy of Isaiah.

"And in that day shall the deaf hear the words of the book, and the eyes of the blind shall see out of obscurity and out of darkness. The meek also shall increase their joy in the Lord and the poor among men shall rejoice in the Holy One of Israel. For the terrible one is brought to nought, and the scorner is consumed, and all that watch for iniquity are cut off: that make a man an offender for a word, and lay a snare for him that reproveth at the gate and turn aside the just for a thing of nought."[99]

---

[99] Isaiah 29: 18-21 (The Open Bible)

The rejection of reproof is actually dangerous because it is what allows us "draw near" to the Father, who is holy. Reproof of our own ways is how we approach holiness. The way parts of society have evolved, hard truths are often rejected as "negative," and the people tasked with presenting the truths are rejected in spite of their honesty and efficacy.

As the fulfillment of this prophecy is realized, what fundamental skills and needs can be framed so that funding can be appropriated for those who need help. Unity of faith helps to synergize effort toward the ultimate goals of healing and wholeness that lead to abundant life.

"And he gave some apostles, and some prophets, and some evangelists and some pastors and teachers for the perfecting of the saints, for the work of the ministry, for the edifying of the body of Christ. Till we all come in the unity of the faith, and of the knowledge of the Son of God, unto a perfect man, unto the measure of the stature of the fullness of Christ: that we be no more children tossed to and fro, and carried about with every wind of doctrine, by the sleight of men, and cunning craftiness whereby they lie in wait to deceive; but speaking the truth in love may grow up into him in all things, which is the head, even Christ from whom the whole body fitly joined together and compacted by that which every joint supplieth, according to the effectual working in the

measure of every part, maketh increase of the body unto the edifying of itself in love.[100]

What I present in the following pages is my effort to create a less esoteric doctrine with conceptual approaches that are both proactive and restorative. This approach facilitates the independence of a person trying to reach to the Father while having concrete goals of personal growth.

If families are strengthened and true faithfulness in The ONE is restored, some jobs may no longer be necessary to the degree thy are now? If there are fairer lending practices, there may be no need for the predatory pay day advance option. We have to get out of this box of *normal.*

A binary perspective of existence, good versus evil, or normal versus abnormal reveals our understanding of the reality that we don't know what we don't know. The discovery of radio waves and how to use them was unknown at one point though those waves were clearly already in existence.

It brings rest to understand that the many things outside of our control are being wisely managed and maintained by that which is greater than all. This highlights the necessity to promote eternal truth so that the transition from reliance on church structure to reliance on the Father can truly be realized.

*"A wonderful and horrible thing is committed in the land;
the prophets prophesy falsely, and the priests bear rule by*

---

[100] Ephesians 4: 11-16 (The Open Bible)

their means; and my people love to have it so: **and what will ye do in the end thereof?**"[101]

When the end of false doctrine comes, how do we measure the trial of our own faith? Since it only takes faith the size of a mustard seed[102] to *move mountains*, trial of it is treacherous and difficult. This contributes to the narrowness of the path and why there are only few who find it.

But we truly need to be tried for our faith to be strengthened. Because of the droves of false teachers and skewed doctrines, it's easy to get caught or preyed on by those you thought were there to help you.

In Matthew 23: 15, Christ admonished religious leaders who ended up making more servants of hell in their efforts to convert others. The necessity of constant learning and refinement of character and understanding in a fallen world cannot be overstated.

The wilderness of religion and doctrine coupled with the fallacy of man in practice necessitate an account of what our true foundations are. The contrast provided in this trial of faith really allows us to assess our true desires.

However, many of our desires are illusive in nature and often come from poor teaching and/or coping strategies. As we turn the corner, we must assess our way of *treating* each other.

---

[101] Jeremiah 5: 30-31 (The Open Bible)
[102] Matthew 17: 20 (The Open Bible)

People take time to heal from the many traumas they experience in life. In a country like the United States, the toxicity of the culture allows most people to experience secondary trauma through the media at least. That doesn't include all the violence, abandonment, neglect, abuse, etc. that people experience in their personal lives, some of which is entertainment.

How many times are victims emotionally victimized because they go unheard and/or unseen? Often people claiming healing power continually injure the injured through a misunderstanding of their pain. Empathy is a skill that needs to be developed. Knowledge and empathy can transform condemnation into edification.

I wonder how well we've considered the perspective of those in pain. Have we considered the efficacy of our labels deeply? Does a person diagnosed with a psychological disorder excuse their behavior or negate a pursuit toward intrinsic motivation to be better because they feel hopeless?

Having spoken with several therapists and counselors, I've recounted childhood trauma over and over. The response to some of the horrible stories I lived was another verbalization to me of how bad it all was as if I didn't know. I've heard about how great it is to let it out and talk about it, but to what end?

I have come to understand that we need to offer much more healing for people that suffer severe emotional wounds. Being heard after the fact doesn't fill the vacuum left in the hearts of victims of severe trauma. Are the lessons learned by the pain subject to the scrutiny of those who cannot empathize?

Empathy can be crucial to actually helping true healing to occur. Often, we learn to cope with emotional pain that doesn't heal because we, and others, focus more on the symptoms of the pain than its causes. We often find fixes for the symptoms as opposed to finding solutions to the problems. And very often, we get masks for the problems from those who have experience only through listening and observation.

Observation is a limited form of assessment; some effects have multiple causes. Are we so certain of our knowledge and observation that we don't value the input of others including, and especially, the victims?

I believe that the vacuum created by ignoring vital specificities decreases the efficacy of some of our interventions. I've been told many times to "let it go" but, an understanding of the sources of one's own trauma does not equate to holding on to it.

The "learning" that takes place during trauma must be replaced with new knowledge the does not confirm what was learned in trauma. The deficit of the knowledge of a different outcome can't come from only having heard of something without experiencing the truth of that thing. For example, I know I can trust the Lord of the Universe. Though my trust in him is great, experience tells me not to trust any people. Until I learn what people can be trusted, this will continue to be an area of growth for me.

Healing is difficult to accomplish without addressing that which caused the malady. The knowledge created by experiences opposite the traumatic ones can help to facilitate this healing. This is where things can be tricky. It is necessary to know what the victim "took away" or "learned" as a result of the trauma. For example, growing up I learned that women despised men and they (women) could never be satisfied.

No one ever taught me that. I observed it to be true from what I observed as a child. As a young man in relationships, this information was confirmed. Or so I thought! Not understanding my own deficits prevented me from truly seeing things clearly. Observation without engagement or interaction is incomplete. Conclusions based on incomplete observations are unreliable.

If true healing and therapy are what we're after, we must dig deeper. We need to learn to teach the truth about how to find that which fills the gap. I believe this already happens, but it needs to happen exponentially more.

There are varying levels of healing, especially as emotional wounds can take longer to heal than physical ones. The primary filler of the gap is the Father of All. This makes the true priest of the Father valuable to the people because of his/her true spiritual insight. Often the necessary tools of healing are both spiritual and natural.

True priests can access the synergy of the spiritual and the natural by the appointment and will of the Father. I believe that the proliferation of hired priestly figures has created a vacuum around true healing. Undoubtedly, many mental health related ailments are trauma-related spiritual and emotional symptoms. As such, focusing on observable symptoms alone can distract from diagnosing the true cause of illness.

Do we have the stomach to hear what we think is irrational long enough to understand and challenge it? We, ideally, wouldn't want to challenge it in an adversarial manner, but fundamentally. Then, are we ready to accept an inability to recognize that which is unknown or unbelievable? How can the imagination merge with reality if what is experienced negates or even places that which one imagines out of reach?

How much does our effort to "treat" people rest in our own vanity as a society? The idiosyncrasies of some victims can make it difficult to be patient with them as they heal. Often our "shoulds" get in the way of the objective truths that can lead to thorough healing.

Sometimes the contributions to sickness are the more manipulative efforts to convince victims of trauma that they don't really hurt or that they shouldn't. Condemnation of the lack ability to recover fast enough is also a way that some illnesses don't heal.

Sometimes the question becomes one of patience. Enduring our own self-evaluation can be rough, especially as we try to recover from trauma. We are often left with scars that obscure some of the best parts of ourselves. Can we make it to the other side and see value in what's left of ourselves?

Have we investigated the ways in which secondary trauma and environment factors into our ability to heal. If certain conditions persist, our approach to healing must seek to negate the impact of environmental factors. This can be dangerous and numbing if it's even possible.

In some ways, our codification of patterns, related symptoms, and connections blinds us to what is right in front of us. While everything may fit established patterns, treatment must be specific to the circumstances. This is where we lack. Some of the things people do are the things they've conditioned themselves to do to receive love and attention.

Though injustice of some kind is the cause of much of our trauma, understanding ourselves and the impacts of the trauma specific to us can lead to healing. Our pace in this technology driven environment can be antithetical to truly examining these things. For each person willing to do the work, healing is available and forgiveness within reach.

I believe we've tried to manufacture the healing unnaturally in our "conveyer belt style" mental health system. Real healing requires real truth. Empathy can occur truly when objective truth is known; to know is complex and beyond cerebral.

The varying perspectives and opinions that we carry evolve over time. As such, our actions do too. Therefore, sometimes, resolution of the past in relationships can happen as we reconcile maturity. Healing often requires reconciliation of the past with the present. Reconciliation can help us to see each other better; this aids empathy.

Seeing ourselves truly is of paramount importance. Often our expectations are what define what is traumatic for us. Our expectations of others may not always match what they do. This trauma can be hard to heal from. Patience with self and others can synergize the healing process in these cases.

We must realize that what works for one patient may not work for another. We are each interpreting the world as we see it. Reconciliation and empathy should work together. We need to get on the same page, so our communications are fruitful.

In some ways, our failure to reconcile has confused our understanding of each other's points of view. Labels and norms have aided in this difficulty because our knowledge and understanding about something may not match its truth.

Having honest conversations can expose vulnerabilities that we often avoid. Addressing them is the place of true healing. The place where we pursue our own inherent goodness and attempt to connect with the founder of it.

Do we know who we are without the labels and false lessons of trauma? Can we be authentic within our own mind? Others aren't aware of our pain, even when we tell them. So, what do we tell ourselves and is it REALLY true?

Living according to the truth does not require us to accept static positions that expose weakness in a given moment. As the moment passes, strength can be the ultimate take away as new knowledge can guide us to strengthen the weaknesses.

For example, I may do something immature, but the behavior itself doesn't define me as immature. I may be immature about that thing or issue, but it doesn't have to define all of who I am. While we all make bad choices from time to time, we still need to focus on the underlying issues that cause our undesired behaviors.

This requires us to look at expectations. Should we expect things from places just because we want them? Adjusting our expectations and looking at situations more thoroughly can help us to improve our own behaviors and/or responses to the behaviors of others.

The expectations that we have developed because of incomplete information make it hard to change course, especially with so many unknowns. Furthermore, you can't throw out the baby with the bath water. Using the same analogy, though, we are the baby. Our heavenly Father knows that we are largely helpless. If we truly balance that fact with our ambitions, we might find it easier to rest as our Father truly care for his children.

CHAPTER 11

Know Better: Reframing

"Whoever loves truth, whoever touches truth, touches the Father's mouth, because truth is the Father's mouth. His tongue is the Holy Spirit, and from his tongue one will receive the Holy Spirit. This is the manifestation of the Father and his revelation to his eternal realms. He revealed his hidden self and explained it. For who has anything within if not the Father alone?"[103]

Given the importance of knowledge to our thoughts, we must ensure that we recover from the errors in our knowledge that we might worship the Lord in spirit and in truth. Knowledge is highly spoken of in scripture for many reasons; our knowledge is linked to our understanding which impacts what we do. This basic premise underpins the cognitive-behavioral model which is, simply put: thoughts lead to feelings that lead to actions. I believe this process to be a bit more complex than that.

While the current cognitive-behavioral model does account for a continuous flow, the breaking down of specific components of thoughts, feelings, and actions adds the impact of past, present, and future knowledge and how it impacts our

---

[103] The Gospel of Truth (Meyer, 2007)

lives overall. For example, if I'm a survivor of sexual abuse or assault and I *learned* that sexual behaviors were the primary way to show love, it may be sometime before my knowledge of love is reframed in a way that helps me to understand that my flawed perception of love influenced the belief that the presence or absence of physical affection corresponded to the presence or absence of love from someone.

This flawed knowledge impacted the ability to recognize thoughts, feelings, and actions of love. As such, right or accurate knowledge is an important tool in the effort to achieve true wholeness.

The cognitive behavioral model that I present depicts how <u>input leads to output</u> with behaviors filtered through our mental constructs. (See figure 1.1, on the next page) The dashed lines in the diagram work in conjunction with the arrows to represent the continuous flow of our minds as we are continually receiving input. Input is received constantly through the five senses, depicted by the icon in the center, and our interactions with others.

While I have identified a few broad categories that should be considered when observing the components of output, most often our inputs are received in small doses depicted by the black dots inside the circle.

Until these inputs are organized, they move about in our minds like noise, and they can occasionally affect output. Though our habits and routines can help to strain unwanted outputs, we are all tasked with being active participants in our own maturity and behavior.

Sometimes these inputs, (represented by black dots in the model), are false knowledge or error. The broad categories in the model are not in any particular order though I've begun with knowledge because it impacts each of the other areas. After knowledge it is important to understand that we interpret inputs differently and our interpretations affect our beliefs and experiences in a cyclic manner.

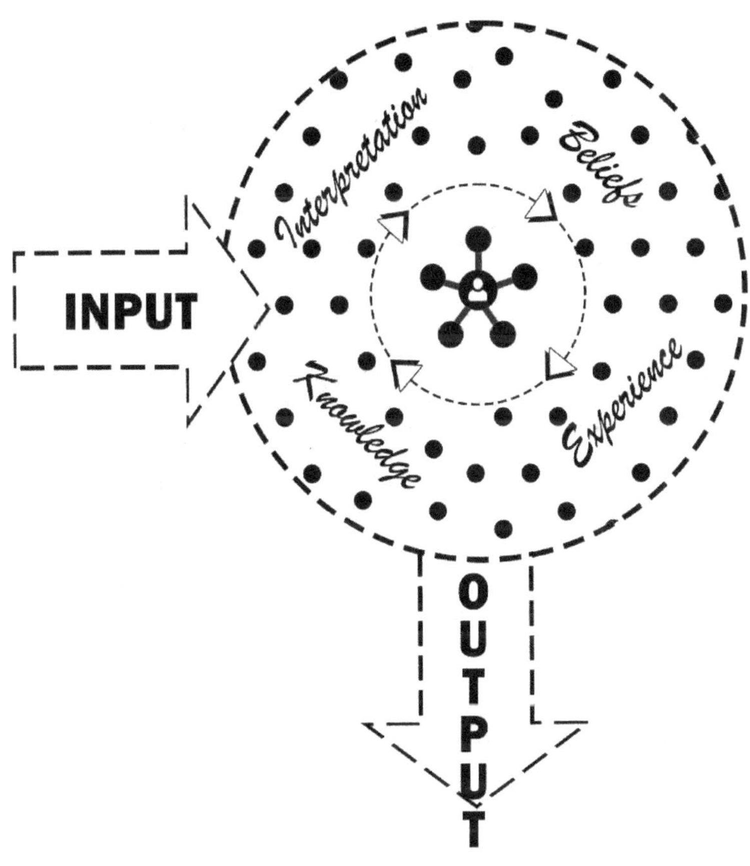

Interpretation — "involves dealing with communication as a configuration of ideas whose comprehension may require a reordering of the ideas into a new configuration in the mind of the individual. This also includes thinking about the relative importance of the ideas, their interrelationships, and their relevance to the generalization implied or described in the original communication. Evidence of interpretation behavior may be found in the inferences, generalizations, or summarizations produced by the individual." (Bloom, p. 90)

Experiences are a very complex component of our mental construct. Though events in time can appear pretty factual and concrete, our experience of life is filtered through our understandings generated by interaction with our environment.

Our experience is often a reflection of our comprehension of various inputs. As such, it can be quite fluid as well since new knowledge and experience can impact our understanding. According to Bloom, translation, interpretation, and extrapolation are comprehension behaviors.

Comprehension – "when students are confronted with communication, they are expected to know what is being communicated and to be able to make some use of the material or ideas contained in it. The communication may be in oral or written form, in verbal or symbolic form, or, if we allow relatively broad use of the term *communication,* it may refer to material in concrete form as well as to material embodied on paper. The term comprehension includes those objectives, behaviors, or responses which represent an understanding of the literal message contained in a communication. In reaching such understanding, the student may change the communication in his mind or in his overt responses to some parallel form more meaningful to him. There may also be responses that represent simple extensions beyond what is given in the communication itself." (Bloom, p. 89)

This constant processing of experiences allows us to categorize our understandings and knowledge into a belief system. From our system of beliefs, we make judgments about past, present and future situations. A more technical term for this is extrapolation. This is a crucial skill in all circumstances as it helps us to plan and respond to the ebb and flow of life.

Extrapolation – "includes the making of estimates or predictions based on the understanding of the trends, tendencies, or conditions described in the communication." (Bloom, p. 90)

In the technical approach I'm taking at this point, especially with the cognitive behavioral model, I've saved translation for last. Poor translations have largely been the catalyst for poor application. Translation relates most readily to the experience category in the model since it is from our experiences that we derive meaning in life.

Rigidity in how we contextualize and translate our experiences can work against us. The difference between caution and fear, for example, cannot be divorced from the context of the situation and the state of mind of the individual. Certain behaviors may look the same but be very different.

> Translation – "means that an individual can put communication into another language, into other terms, or into another form of communication. It will usually involve the giving of meaning to various parts of communication, taken in isolation, although such meanings may in part be determined by the context in which the ideas appear." (Bloom, pp. 89-90)

The second chapter of the book of Judges describes the pattern that the Lord used with his people, even before it had been written. After the conversion of Abraham,

> *"...the unwritten Torah was named among them and the works of the commandments were then fulfilled and belief in the coming judgment was then generated and hope of the world that was to be renewed was then built up and*

the promise of the life that should come hereafter was implanted."[104]

Embedded in these pages is knowledge that reframes some of the written foundational language in a more accurate, spiritual way that reflects a different approach than much of Christian theology in practice. Consider that the quote above describes the unwritten way of the Lord.

Until the manifestation of the rest that is promised, Christ prepared his listeners to be persecuted for righteousness' sake and told true believers that they were already blessed. In a way, *blessings* have been reframed to indicate receipt of things external rather than the state of being one is already in. Consider the conversation Yeshua had with "the rich young ruler" when he told him that being *perfect* would require him to give all his goods to the poor.

Though our Father allows us to acquire *things*, they do not alone define our relationship with him, and we should be careful of the place we give the things we acquire. We must be sure that we aren't being controlled subconsciously by our pursuit of more stuff which we, in some ways, begin to worship as our sovereign.

"Proclaiming matter sole and autocratic sovereign
of the boundless universe, they would forcibly

---

[104] 2 Baruch 57: 2 (Et Cepher 3rd Edition)

divorce her from her consort, and place the widowed queen on the great throne of nature made vacant by the exiled spirit. And now, they try to make her appear as attractive as they can by incensing and worshipping at the shrine of their own building. Do they forget or are they utterly unaware of the fact, that in the absence of its legitimate sovereign, this throne is but a whited sepulcher inside of which all is rottenness and corruption! That *matter* without the *spirit* which vivifies it, and of which it is but the "gross purgation," to use a hermetic expression, is nothing but a soulless corpse, whose limbs, in order to be moved in predetermined directions, require an intelligent operator at the great galvanic battery called life." (Blavatsky, 1888, p. 103)

A change in our priorities that reflects our Father's point of view is precisely what Christ advocated for. In many ways, the beatitudes are declarations of the true state of certain conditions that may not appear as they truly are. For example, it is often quite offensive when someone reviles you and lies on you especially when you've done something right. Christ says this is great and that you are blessed. As such, our response to others matures to reflect greater understanding of this.

This vision or sight is spiritual in nature and is very much a part of Christ's declaration from Isaiah chapter 60 where the recovery of sight to the blind was also fulfilled with his teaching or *gospel*. Rejection of the word of the Lord and his servants by his people is also a part of the pattern experienced by Moses, Joshua, and Samuel just to name a few. But just as the Lord told Samuel, the people did not reject him (Samuel), but they rejected the Lord.[105]

Many of those chosen by the Lord were rejected by the people because the people preferred ways other than those the Lord prescribed. In some cases, they chose the ways of the other nations that were around them, often idolaters. Sometimes the man of God was threatened by the people because of the word he was given to deliver.

This pattern exceeded focus on any one person but rather the Father of us all. This creates our challenge going forward as we must realign our perspectives which must begin with the reframing of our collective knowledge and perspective on the law or commandments. "Law" is a poor word choice to describe all that the Torah and the commandments represent.

The commandment does not itself condemn. Man condemns himself when his heart's desire is contrary to the law or Torah. Because the heart is deceitfully wicked, one must purify desires from within making the Holy Spirit a necessity. The spirit of the Lord aids spiritual servants as they diagnose the root causes of sickness spiritually.

---

[105] 1 Samuel 8:7 (The Open Bible)

The commandments gave contrast to the abhorrent behaviors nations and people had especially having come out of Egypt. These behaviors, in many ways, displeased the Lord, not the people. Consider how many of the Israelites worshipped the Golden Calf as their deliverer because of their idolatry and impatience.

What harm can come from the honor due to parents? Why would someone want to misrepresent what they saw and become a false witness? The answers to those questions are quite complex. Free will allows us to make choices as we will but those choices reveal the condition of our hearts. What do we crave? Do we know why we make the choices we make? What do they truly show us about our unperceived deficiencies? I've often wondered what was so hard about keeping the commandments. I realize now that vanity is the primary reason!

The command to love our neighbor as ourselves poses no mortal threat; what is the opposition to this based on? Because we live in a society that has thrived on division and illusions, in some ways, we don't realize how much weaker we are without unity. The ups and downs that we all experience in life are helped by each other's flexibility and patience. It is more efficient for us to work together!

Multiplicity occurs in the natural harmony of diversity; we don't have to create it in some false, deceptive way. Explaining me is different than convincing you; boasting and bragging about our Father is a part of me. I don't have to compel anyone to agree with me because what I believe, I know to be true.

"As the name of a man clings to him, so men cling to names. For the primitive savage, the name is part of the essence of a person or thing and even in the more advanced stages of culture, judgments are not always formed in agreement with the facts as they are, but rather according to the names by which they are called." (Ginzberg, p. Preface)

To this point, I've used pronouns such as we and he and I have used what is a commonly viewed gender-specific term: father. However, the one Christ referred to as *"our Father"* is greater than can be described. I quote here from *scripture* found at Nag Hammadi that presents a perspective of *Our Father* that is greater in detail and different than any passage in the bible.

"The One is the Invisible Spirit. We should not think of it as a god or like a god. For it is greater than a god, because it has nothing over it and no lord above it. It does not exist within anything inferior to it, since everything exists within it, for it established itself. It is eternal, since it does not need anything, for it is absolutely complete. It has never lacked anything in order to be completed by it. Rather, it is always absolutely complete in light.

The One is:

Illimitable,
since there is nothing before it to limit it

Unfathomable,
since there is nothing before it to fathom it

Immeasurable,
since there was nothing before it to measure it

Invisible, since nothing has seen it

Eternal, since it exists eternally

Unutterable,
since nothing could comprehend it to utter it

Unnamable,
since there is nothing before it to name it"[106]

As we see in this passage, the pronoun used by Christ, the speaker in the text, to describe the *Father* is ***it.*** How different is it from Christian theology to think of the one Christ spoke of and taught about to be described the way we describe average *things*!?

We've become so attached to the actual word *god* that often we assume we all mean the same thing. In this way, the true essence of names must be recaptured and renewed. Just as

---

[106] The Secret Book of John (Meyer, 2007)

language was the tool used to dismantle truth, the reproof of our understanding of spiritual language can begin the repair of our faith in practice.

The words *Allah* and *Eloah* mean the exact same thing, the former being Aramaic and the latter Hebrew; they both refer to *The One* but are not attempts to name it. This is the same *"one"* Christ was speaking of! When we look at scripture closely in its original language, these are the words we find, not *god*. It this way, the Hellenization of scripture has obscured these basic truths that are understood in religions other than mainstream Christianity.

Wayne Grudem defines systematic theology as any study that answers the question, "What does the whole Bible teach us today?"[107] This approach leaves Christian doctrine and theology wanting as it has gotten tunnel-vision with the scriptures that refer to other scriptures whose relevance has often been decided based on popularity.

Correction and reproof are often not very popular and many apocryphal scriptures, along with other scriptures, require a proper view of their relevance rather than the wholesale rejection of their contents. If the *all* of 2 Timothy 3:16-17 is truly believed, we can better scrutinize the relevance of these scriptures with *fresh* eyes as opposed to continually affirming the medieval goal of clandestine control of spiritual activity.

---

[107] Bible Doctrine (Grudem, p. 17)

For me, this calls into question the *Holy Bible* itself. It does not represent the whole of our communication with *The One* and is limited in scope. A complete translation of the "Holy Bible" into English, completed in 1382, was based on the Latin Vulgate. John Wycliffe, who translated though, was a reformer before what officially became known as the Protestant Reformation.

He spoke out sharply against the depravity in the church and some of its doctrines that were not rooted in scripture. His foundational belief and reform lay in the belief that scripture had and has greater authority than man's traditions. While many English people gladly received the new Bible, Pope John XXIII is recorded as saying, "this pestilent and wretched John Wycliffe of cursed memory, that son of the old serpent." (Arnold, p. 46)

In *On the Truth of Scriptures*, Wycliffe repeatedly defends the authenticity and authority of scripture understood in the "true sense." In Part One he vehemently expresses disdain for the interpretation of scripture that is only literal and is void of the true nature intended.

"…still this modern generation, intent on seeking after signs (Matt. 16:4), devotes its attention chiefly to this aspect of scripture, despite the fact that what it possesses is no more fittingly considered scripture than the lines on a hand discerned in palm reading, or the configuration of points for prognosticating from the earth. Indeed, it amounts to no more than the trace of a tortoise shell upon a rock, except

insofar as it is exemplified by the prior scripture. Under no circumstances is it deemed sacred, except for the fact that it functions as a guiding process which leads the faithful into knowledge of the heavenly scripture. For this reason it is considered holy in an even more remote fashion than vestments and other priestly ornaments are said to be holy. Strip away that sense and you will see that what remains is holy, for the aggregate is Holy Scripture." (Wycliffe, p. 102)

Unfortunately, his admonition to be guided by the Holy Spirit in interpreting scripture got him labeled a heretic in a true Christ-like fashion. It is also worth noting that after Wycliffe's natural death, his remains were exhumed, burned, and thrown into a nearby stream. Others that helped with his project were jailed or were burned at the stake with the new bible tied around their neck.[108] These behaviors, guided by the papacy, cemented a change in the trajectory of spiritual education.

Quite often the "Holy Bible" became a tool to manage large groups of people. Our common KJV came about primarily to reframe scriptural translation to strengthen the monarchy as "God's chosen form of government." Clearly, if they needed to revise the true text to fit a narrative while being beautifully elegant with the language as to be competitive with other versions, truth would be lost, especially since it was

---

[108] (Arnold, 2008)

already largely unknown. This *error* helped to create a new counterfeit consciousness of God's will despite the scriptures to the contrary.

Because writings have survived many revisions, translations, and applications, what we deem *scripture* can be subjective as those bound to specific practices of faith view "sacred" writings of other faith practices as potentially wicked. Even bible burning was popular at one time due to all of the competing versions of it in circulation. But this was not new either.

In the book of Jeremiah 8: 8, the Lord is reprimanding the children of Judah for another instance of their violation of the covenant and mentions the scribes' error referring to them (the scribes) as liars who were leading the children into error. If even those who wrote what we deem scripture were possibly lying, we really need to be more careful. This cannot be overstated!

As earlier I shared basics of how our knowledge has impacted our religious education, because of all that has been mentioned, our comprehension or understandings need to be readjusted. Our translation, interpretation, and extrapolations based on scriptures in the application of our faith in *The One* will be scrutinized more carefully going forward in a solution-based way.

"Competence in translation is dependent on the possession of the requisite or relevant knowledge.
It is also true that unless an individual can give the

denoted meaning to each of the various parts of a communication and/or in terms of immediate or adjacent context, he will be unable to engage in more complex thinking about the communication. For such thinking, a given term in a communication must symbolize for the individual a general concept or even an aggregate of relevant ideas. An abstract idea may need to be transformed to concrete or everyday terms to be useful in further thinking about some problem presented by the communication." (Bloom, p. 91)

If we learn more thoroughly and truly, we can apply the concepts found in scripture to our own lives. In this way, our testimonies can do more to demonstrate empathy and faith than our attempts to teach doctrine. Often, the reason we recount past victories in the face of adversity is to encourage ourselves to rely on the Lord.

Examples of this are present throughout scripture. Looking carefully at Psalm 42, the psalmist directs himself to remember and hope in Yah. This approach is helpful because it is an approach of *tehillah* and *tephillah*. Here I've used the Hebrew translations for praise and prayer respectively. While the word *psalms* can accurately describe prayers or praises set to music, Psalms 1-72 are more accurately described as prayers or *tephillah*. (Strong, p. 893)

"In order to interpret a communication, the reader must first of all be able to translate each of the major parts of it – this includes not only the words and phrases, but also the various representational devises used. He must then be able to go beyond this part for part rendering of the communication to comprehend the relationships between its various parts, to reorder, or to rearrange it in his mind so as to secure some total view of what the communication contains and to relate it to his own fund of experiences and ideas. Interpretation also includes competence in recognizing the essentials and differentiating them from the less essential portions or from the relatively irrelevant aspects of the communication." (Bloom, p. 93)

This intimate look into David's thoughts through his prayers in Psalm 42 reveal a paradox of state of mind and emotion. How effective would it have been for someone observing his disquietude to *minister* to him apart from the Lord's direct, clear instruction to them? He knew how to minister to himself! The Father always provided his needs despite much difficulty and if there was any attempt to minister to him, it would really just be an attempt to change his disposition.

How often have our attempts to *minister* to people actually just been a vain desire to see someone be something they're not – like happy? Maybe they are happy and just show it differently. Though we say we appreciate diversity, it seems we have trouble responding honestly to things that are different or don't exist as *we* think they should.

"In preparing a communication, the writer attempts not only to state what he believes the truth of the matter to be, but also some of the consequences of it. While occasionally the writer is exhaustive, has detailed all of the conclusions to be drawn, and has indicated all of the possible consequences or implication of his ideas or material, this is rarely the case.

Accurate extrapolation requires that the reader be able to translate as well as interpret the document, and in addition, he must be able to extend the trends or tendencies beyond the given date and findings of the document to determine implication, consequences, corollaries, effects, etc. which are in accordance with the conditions as literally described in the original communication. Extrapolation requires that the reader be well aware of the limits within which the communication is posed as well as the possible limits within which it can be extended. In practically all cases, the reader must recognize that extrapolation can only be an inference which has some degree of probability – certainty with respect to extrapolation is rare." (Bloom, p. 95)

Going forward we need to really be careful that we remain patient and present in our interactions. Allowing others to truly *be* can mean accepting comfort and discomfort while being honest and responsive in the moment. This perspective reminds us to walk alongside others as we, too, are walking with the Father. Throughout the course of the *walk,* we experience faithfulness as the Father doesn't abandon us though we stumble on some of the terrain of life.

We must remember, then, that true edification is experienced differently as an individual versus as in a group. Corporate worship and the building of a social network of like-minded individuals is a beautiful thing. We just need to acknowledge the way that our practices reflect condemnation and compulsion instead of reconciliation and humility. This effort must begin with a proper framing of the Holy Bible.

The use of the Bible as a representation of the *Word of God* represents just a small fraction of what that, (*the Word of God*), entails. 1 Samuel 3:1 describes the *word of the Lord* as being *precious* in those days, the basic idea behind this verse being that communications from the Lord were not *a dime a dozen* and it truly was a special thing to truly hear from the Lord of creation. Furthermore, the "word of God" was not something written but represented that which was expected to be acted upon in all its complexity. His *word* represents an expression of his will.

Consider the song in the foreword of this book. In this *song,* the three operations of his words are clear yet complex. Take notice of the fact that *"word"* is plural throughout the song! Christ also understood and declared that he did not exist apart from that which was before him and that the words he spoke were given to him by his Father, THE ONE.[109] This is important because a foundational premise of the Christian church is that the Holy Bible is infallible and itself represents the word of God.

I believe that the main problem or *stumbling block* that the Bible presents in its current form is **how** we have come to *use* it. In some cases, our inheritance of error has caused us to compartmentalize and abuse scripture in vain ways instead of truly seeking the Lord for his *living* word for us today! As the following quote shows, this has been the case for centuries and our Father is so faithful to us in making us aware of our error so that we can truly worship him with our lives in spirit and in truth.

"The entirety of the evil which is so thoroughly infecting Christendom arises from forsaking the sense of *scripture* which is keeping with that form which Christ instituted…

---

[109] Gospel of John 17 (The Open Bible)

By mutilating Holy scripture, heretics deny that it is true. Not conceding it in its wholeness, they interpret it as they like, thereby twisting it to suit their own perverse sense, then seeking the aid of secular lords to foment their crime." (Wycliffe, 2001)

The Doctrine of Discovery, mentioned earlier, is only one such example of proof of John Wycliffe's statements. There are other fundamental bits of knowledge that have been skewed in practice that have perpetuated fatherlessness, widowhood, and divorce, just to name a few of societies' ills. Furthermore, it would take an in-depth study and juxtaposition of church culture, much scripture, and popular culture to discover how the Bible and its interpretations have impacted what we do to each other and how we treat one another.

Some act as if being *born again* means that they don't have to experience the consequences of their choices. Resurrection is a change in condition, not identity. The changes in behavior and choices are born from the desire to live and not die *spiritually*.

Philippians chapter three begins with identification and clarification for those endeavoring to walk in the spirit that we have no confidence in the flesh. This death of fleshly perspective creates room to *attain unto the resurrection of the dead.*[110] We leave the priorities of our fleshly existence to focus on that part of us that is living and eternal.

> *"You show great acts to those who know you not; you break up the enclosure of those who are ignorant and light up what is dark and reveal what is hidden to the pure who in faith have submitted themselves to you and your Torah."*[111]

We've become accustomed to the use of names, some of which are pronouns, to describe the Almighty. In some cases, Christian churches demand that Jesus' name be given complete supremacy though that is contrary to what he said.

> *"And now I am no more in the world, but these are in the world, and I come to thee. Holy Father, **keep through thine own name** those whom thou hast given me, that they may be one, as we are."*[112]

As I have attempted in this work to add proper perspective to some common spiritual language, I have only scratched the surface. Digging deeper as we go forward, my goal is to provide the knowledge and perspective necessary for our transition from error.

---

[110] Philippians 3:11 (The Open Bible)
[111] 2 Baruch 54:5 (Et Cepher 3rd Edition)
[112] Gospel of John 17:11 (The Open Bible)

As I said earlier, I want to expose truths related to the word *Hallelujah*. This common word of praise, when studied closely, reveals much deceit yet provides additional reasons for praise. "The word *halal* is the source of *Hallelujah,* a Hebrew expression of *praise* to God which has taken over into virtually every language of mankind." (Strong, p. 430) In this way, a more appropriate translation for the word psalms, a Greek expression, would be a book of *praises*. The book of Psalms is also referred to as *tehilliym* or deeds worthy of praise.

The word *tehilliym*, plural of *tehillah*, also has *halal* as its root. In fact, "Psalms 113-118 are traditionally referred to as the "Hall-el Psalms" because they have to do with praise to God for deliverance from Egyptian bondage under Moses." (Strong, p. 430) The deceit hidden in the knowledge and use of this word comes from the translation and interpretation of this same expression in Isaiah 14:12 of the King James Version.

The King James Version, along with many other versions of the Bible, translate the equivalent of the Hebrew *hall-el* with Lucifer. Great effort has gone into characterizing this servant of the Father under chastisement as evil. Look closely at how the Tanakh, a non-Hellenized translation of scripture, translates Isaiah 14:12:

> *"How are you fallen from heaven, O Shining One, son of Dawn! How are you felled to earth, O vanquisher of nations!"*

This error in interpretation and understanding has impacted religious and civil discourse in more ways than are publicly known! In truth, it reveals the fact that there is no respect of persons with the Father. All of those he loves, he chastens.[113] This brings me comfort because it reveals the justice at every level of the Father's creation.

But the effort to vilify a righteous servant of the Lord under chastisement also reveals a lack of understanding of the power of praise. *Halal* means to shine, to be clear, or to boast in Hebrew. The power of praise is that it is an expression of boasting in the Father's name or reputation.

This response is often an excited utterance that represents the pinnacle of verbal expression towards the Most High. Though not represented in many translations of the Psalms, each one begins and or ends with Hallelujah! Consider this editorial comment:

> "Each song ends with "Hallelujah," a stock response by the listener or congregation and probably a scribal addition. The tag is here omitted as unnecessary and distracting from the content and beauty of the poem." (Barnstone & Meyer, p. 378 editorial)

---

[113] Hebrews 12: 6-7 (The Open Bible)

The editor calls Hallelujah a "stock response" and denotes *probably* a scribal addition. This comment reminds me that true praise has been considered irrelevant. This knowledge is fundamental going forward as it will hopefully cause us to really review what we've inherited in word and deed. This can help us to be more honest in our motives as a community of citizens, whether laymen or faith teachers.

"Through wisdom a house is built and by understanding it is established and by knowledge shall the chambers be filled with all precious and pleasant riches. A wise man is strong; yea, man of knowledge increaseth strength. For by wise counsel thou shalt make thy war: and in multitude of counselors there is safety."[114]

If wisdom comes from the Father and is truly one of his first works, the new covenant Christ spoke of to be made in his blood begs the question: what is the blood of a word? I was a voice major in college and the most important thing I learned about producing a healthy tone is how to use my breath.

Without breath, words are unheard outside of the thoughts in which they originate. The significance of this fact in the context of the Father is that breath represents the flow of the *ruwach ha'qodesh* or holy wind; this is synonymous with his holy spirit.

---

[114] Proverbs 24:3-6 (The Open Bible)

"For the word of the Lord is right; his every deed is faithful. He loves what is right and just; the earth is full of the Lord's faithful care. By the word of the Lord the heavens were made, by the breath of his mouth, all their host."[115]

The verse quoted above expresses the power of the spirit of the Lord in creation. When Christ called the group of disciples together after he had been resurrected, he breathed on them.[116] Christ told them at that time to receive the holy ghost. Furthermore, in the last chapter of the book of Luke, Christ tells the disciples to wait for the promise of the Father and the power from on high. This power they experienced in the upper room was not new to them, but the evidence it provided for observers was a catalyst for their ministries.

This gift of the Father's spirit is described by Paul in the first chapter of Ephesians as the *earnest of our inheritance*. This gift of grace through faith via the spirit of the Lord is precisely the fulfillment of the Father's promise to write his law on the *inward parts* of his people.[117] The gospel of Christ was inextricably linked to this plan as those *grafted into the vine* are recipients of the promise by faith.[118] The primary reason for revisiting these things is that Christian practice, namely

---

115 Psalm 33:4-6 (Tanakh: The Holy Scriptures)
116 Gospel of John 20:22 (The Open Bible)
117 Jeremiah 31:33 (The Open Bible)
118 Hebrews 10:10 (The Open Bible)

Church, has evolved without respect to the following part of the promise:

> *"And they shall teach no more every man his neighbor, and every man his brother, saying, Know the Lord: for they shall all know me, from the least of them unto the greatest of them, saith the Lord. For I will forgive their iniquity, and I will remember their sin no more. Thus saith the Lord, which giveth the sun for a light by day, and the ordinances of the moon and of the stars for a light by night, which divideth the sea when the waves thereof roar; The Lord of hosts is his name."*[119]

Because of the proliferation of church, our expectations for the fulfillment of this promise can be awakened. Because growth and maturity are processes that take time, we can help each other to grow personally with truth and honesty. As we come into unity of the faith,[120] we can see the church's role in *scaffolding* us into seeking the Lord. It is still the work of individuals to add faith and knowledge with truth.[121] This topic opens the book of Hebrews which speaks of a better priesthood centered around the Holy Spirit's guidance.

How is it that the meek inherit the earth? Because the meek represent those who have chosen willingly to govern themselves in the true fear of the Lord. It isn't the merit of

---

[119] Jeremiah 31:34 (The Open Bible)
[120] Ephesians 4:13 (The Open Bible)
[121] 2 Peter 1:5-9 (The Open Bible)

behavior that allows us this grace – it is a gift.[122] Though it is a gift, it doesn't negate the impact of an effort to exhibit righteous behavior; the Lord rewards it with life. While we still need each other, the context of our admonitions and *provoking one another to love and good works*[123]must be guided by the Holy Spirit.

> *"Have I any pleasure at all that the wicked should die and not that he should return from his ways and live?"*[124]

As I close this discourse, I want to be clear about how I reframe "the name." *The name of the Lord is a strong tower that the righteous run into and they are safe.*[125] The name of the Lord is declared through the reputation of his works. Though his specific name was not used in the book of Esther, his name was known and shown in his protection of and provision for his people. The trap laid for the people of the Lord, especially his prophet, ended up catching the foot of him who laid it.[126] In his name is also grace and mercy for those who don't know him to learn about.

The word *shem* is the Hebrew word for name that is used 864 times in the Bible. (Strong, p. 857) It is defined through the idea of definite and conspicuous position as a mark of

---

[122] Ephesians 2:8 (The Open Bible)
[123] Hebrews 10:24 (The Open Bible)
[124] Ezekiel 18:23 (The Open Bible)
[125] Proverbs 18:10 (The Open Bible)
[126] Psalm 141:9-10 (The Open Bible)

individuality. It can be a synonym for reputation and fame and comes from a root that means to place something somewhere. Though the Father names us, he also gives us his name. This reminds us of the importance of not *taking his name in vain*.

All things exist according to his *name*, he who keeps truth forever, executes justice for the oppressed and gives bread to the hungry. His *name* and reputation include loosing the prisoners, opening the eyes of the blind, raising up those who are bowed down, preserving the strangers, upholding the fatherless and the widow all while loving the righteous.[127] When we pray and close our prayers out with *"in your name,"* are we referring to this *name*?

I believe the truth is that those of us who pray to the God of Abraham, the Father of our Lord Christ, are speaking to this *One* whether we say God or Allah. Having been raised in the church with *true Christians*, I know that when many people say, *"in Jesus name,"* they too are speaking of this name despite the complexities of error in the doctrine.

I close with a song that exemplifies how this work represents one of the truths of the impact of the breath of the Father on me as I live up to my name by petitioning the Father to *spare it a little longer*. May his *name* be praised!

"As a hand moves over a harp and string speak, so the spirit of the Lord speaks in my members and I speak through his love, for he destroys what is foreign and bitter.

---

127 Psalm 146 (The Open Bible)

So he was from the beginning and so he will contend to the end. No one can remain his adversary or resist him. The Lord multiplies his knowledge. He is zealous to inform us, and he gives through grace. Through his name we apprehend praise, and our spirits praise his Holy Spirit.

A stream erupts into a wide and endless river that floods and, breaking, carries away the temple. Ordinary men, and even those whose art is to stem tough waters, cannot hold it back, and the river covers the face of the whole earth. The river fills everything, and the thirsty of the earth drink and satisfy thirst. The drink comes from the highest one.

Blessings on the ministers of that drink, who guard his waters that assuage dry lips and raise the fainted Souls about to depart, his waters rescue from death and straighten crooked limbs. They strengthen our feebleness and feed our eyes with light. Those who know the river of the Lord live through it forever."[128]

---

[128] Odes of Solomon (Barnstone & Meyer, 2003,2009)

Works Cited

Al-Ghazali, A. H. (2010). *The Savior from Error.* Ft. Lauderdale, FL: Al-Baz Publishing.

Al-Ghazali, I. (2016). *On Disciplining the Soul.* Great Shelford, Cambridge: The Islamic Texts Society.

American Heritage Dictionary of the English Language. (1969). New York, NY: American Heritage Publishing Co.

Arnold, C. (2008). *How We Got the Bible.* Grand Rapids, MI: Zondervan.

Barnstone, W., & Meyer, B. (2003,2009). *The Gnostic Bible.* Boulder, Colorado: Shambhala Publications.

Blavatsky, H. (1877). *Isis Unveiled.* Monee, IL: Pantianos Classics.

Blavatsky, H. (1888). *The Secret Doctrine.* Theosophical University Press.

Bloom, B. S. (1956). *Taxonomy of Educational Objectives: Thae Classification of Educational Goals.* New York: David McKay Company Inc.

Charles, M., & Rah, S.-C. (2019). *Unsettling Truths: The Ongoing Dehumaninzing Legacy of the Doctrine of Discovery.* Downers Grove, Illinois: InterVarsity Press.

Charles, R. H. (1912). *Fragments of a Zadokite Work.* Cambridge, MA: Oxford at the Clarendon Press.

Churton, T. (2021). *Lost Pillars of Enoch.* Rochester, VT: Churton.

Churton, T. (2021). *The Lost Pillars of Enoch.* Rochester, Vermont: Inner Traditions.

Diprose, R. E. (2000). *Israel and the Church: The Origins and Effects of Replacement Theology.* Rome, Italy: Intervarsity Press.

Dubois, W. E. (1903). *The Souls of Black Folk.* Mineola, NY: Dover Publication Inc.

Et Cepher 3rd Edition. (n.d.). Cepher Publishing Group.

Ginzberg, L. (1946). *The Legends of the Jews III.* Jewish Publication Society of America.

Grudem, W. (1999). *Bible Doctrine: Essential Teachings of the Christian Faith.* Grand Rapids, Michigan: Zondervan.

Hall, M. (2007). *The Secret Teachings of All Ages.* Radford, VA: Wilder Publications.

Hall, M. (2008). *The Secret Destiny of America.* Ontario, Canada: Penguin Group.

Hall, M. (2017). *The Ways of the Lonely Ones.* Eastford, CT: The Hall Publishing Company.

Hoeller, S. A. (1982). *The Gnostic Jung and the Seven Sermons to the Dead.* Wheaton, IL: Theosophical Publishing House.

Johnson, K. (2008). *The Ancient Book of Jasher.* Bible Facts Ministries.

Lynch, W. (1712). *The Willie Lynch Letter and the Making of a Slave.*

Meyer, M. (2007). *The Nag Hammadi Scriptures.* New York, New York: HarperCollins Publishers.

Sinnet, A. P. (1885). *Esoteric Buddhism.* Istanbul: eKitap Projesi; Cheapest Books.

Strong, J. L. (2001). *The New Strong's Epanded Dictionary of Bible Words.* Nashville, Tennessee: Thomas Nelson Publishers.

Tanakh: The Holy Scriptures. (1985). The Jewish Publication Society.

The Book of Mormon. (1830). Palmyra, New York: The Church of Jesus Christ of Latter Day Saints.

The Lost Books of the Bible and the Forgotten Books of Eden. (1926; 1927). World Bible Publishers Inc.

The New Oxford Annotated Apocrypha Third Edition. (1989). New York, New York: Oxford University Press.

The Open Bible. (n.d.).

Vermes, G. (1962). *The Complete Dead Sea Scrolls in English.* The Penguin Group.

Washington, J. M. (1986). *A Testament of Hope.* New York, New York: HarperCollins Publishers.

Woodson, C. G. (1933). *The Mis-Education of the Negro.*

Wycliffe, J. (2001). *On the Truth of Holy Scripture.* Kalamazoo, MI: Midieval Institute Publications.

9 789898 541093